Questions People Ask About RELIGION

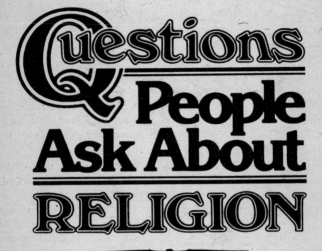

Questions People Ask About RELIGION

W. E. Sangster

Abingdon / Nashville

QUESTIONS PEOPLE ASK ABOUT RELIGION

A Festival Book

Festival edition published February 1980

ISBN 0-687-35160-X

PRINTED IN THE UNITED STATES OF AMERICA

FOREWORD

No one was ever argued into religion; but discussion can do something. It can discover the deep difficulties which people have about religion and put them into precise terms. It can answer them—or cast some light upon them when no complete answer is possible. It can show the greater objections to other answers, and clear away the obstacles to that mental venture which is increasingly recognized as the door to religious conviction. All this it can do—if not to the satisfaction of every questing mind, at least with sincerity and (one hopes) with clearness as well. This I have attempted to do in the pages which follow.

I have tried in particular to help two groups of people: (1) those interested in religion but not yet committed to it; and (2) those committed to religion but not able to show the reasonableness of their position to people who question it. I have written for thoughtful men and women—however advanced in their own profession or calling—who have not had academic training in philosophy or theology. Should my book come into the hands of any in this latter group, they will recognize (I hope) my awareness of the big problems which face us, but understand my care to avoid the technical terms of our specialist studies.

If I have had one class in the community more in mind than another, it is working men (No suggestion that other men don't work!) for whom I have always had a special affection, and whose absence from the Church has been a pain to me for many years. I shall not be content if the book is of use only in church parlors. I hope it may also have a use wherever men meet for fellowship and, sometimes, discuss religion.

The method is simple. I have taken a hundred questions which people have put to me at various times, and have given an answer, of roughly the same length, to each of them. I have tried to set the questions down in such a way that one leads to the next, so that the book could be read here and there (according to the particular interest of the reader) or straight through. Where an answer seems incomplete, the related parts of it may be found elsewhere.

I have tried to write, not from any denominational angle, but of the things most Christians hold in common. I cannot hope to have had a full success in that honest endeavor, but I hope my fellow Christians will regard my effort with understanding. The task of the hour is for stress, not on our denominational differences, but on the world's desperate need for the things we all believe.

No complete outline of Christian theology will be found here; the method I have adopted precludes it. The most intimate things of religion are never really reached. In my experience. people taking their first steps toward faith are not deeply worried about whether there are two Sacraments or seven, or whether the Holy Spirit is personal, or many other questions I could mention. Their early needs relate rather to the things which I have dealt with, and these other questions can wait until they are in fellowship with God's Church in one of its branches.

I am fully aware of the incompleteness of the answers. Lack of space (if nothing else) compels that. I am also aware that some who share my faith would prefer our case put (on occasion) in another way. Yet, despite this, I continue to hope that I shall have some success in my double endeavor—that those uncommitted to religion will venture forward in the ways I advise, and those committed, but unable to explain their position, will feel themselves furnished with some of the facts and reasons on which their faith is built.

My warmest thanks are given to the Rev. Greville P. Lewis, and the Rev. R. E. Davies for their helpful comments on what I have written; to Miss Margaret Gregory for typing the manuscript and, Miss Marie Berry for reading the proofs.

W. E. SANGSTER

CONTENTS

11

JESUS CHRIST

THE BIBLE

PRAYER

PROVIDENCE

THE CHURCH

WHAT COULD CHRIST DO...?

EPILOGUE

1

Do We Need Religion?

BELIEF IN GOD INVOLVES (FOR THE MASS OF MEN AND WOMEN) the practice of religion, but people have sometimes wondered why we need a religion at all. Animals don't worship; why should men?

Men have always worshiped. Explorers have occasionally reported contact with primitive people who appeared to have no religion, but investigation has disproved the appearances. In some form or other, all primitive people believe in a God. Men are not natural atheists; they argue themselves into atheism.

But this, of itself, does not prove the existence of God. It might prove the opposite—that as we get more educated we no longer need "God" to explain things. Yet why are so many educated people deeply religious?

In order to make sense of life. Right at the core of man's mind there is the conviction that life has meaning, that it didn't "just happen," that there is purpose and design in it somewhere—though it be a design hard to distinguish and a purpose not fully clear. Even those people who have given up the hope of finding meaning in life often confess to a haunting conviction that there is sense in it somewhere, and need constantly to tell themselves that they have given up hope!

The religious man feels no need to strangle the intuition of our race that there is meaning in life. He *trusts* the intuition. He *seeks* the meaning. He seeks it in God.

If we want to understand life, we need religion.

2

Does Religion Really Matter?

PEOPLE SOMETIMES ARGUE, NOT THAT RELIGION IS UNTRUE, BUT that it is irrelevant; that it is not closely bound up with life, that it doesn't matter in any large way, that it may have its own interest and, indeed, fascination for those whose "hobby" it is, but that others can cheerfully ignore it and live a complete life. They seem to put it in the same category as stamp collecting—full of interest to those who like it, and all but meaningless to everybody else.

This will not do. The main contentions of religion may be true or false, but if they are true they can't be irrelevant. If God is there, if he has a plan for the universe, if his high statesmanship is over events, if our life goes on after death, and if how we live here has consequences there . . . this isn't stamp collecting! Nothing compares to it in importance—not even the answer to peace and war, or the long-sought cure of cancer.

Deny the central contentions of religion if you must (though do be sure that you are not *wanting* to disbelieve for private reasons) ; hold judgment in suspense if you are compelled (but be certain that you have given the claim of God upon your life serious, intelligent, and unhurried consideration) ; but don't say it doesn't matter, for nothing matters so much.

Suppose for a moment that the claims of religion were true. Entertain in the mind the conviction that behind the universe there is a Great Being, infinite in wisdom and infinite in love, wanting to work out on the earth a sublime purpose in harmony with his nature. Suppose that he is approachable and knowable. . . . If you only *suppose* it, can you say that it wouldn't matter? Nothing else would matter so much.

3

Hasn't Much Evil Been Done by Religion?

YES, IT HAS. RELIGION HAS BEEN USED TO HINDER EDUCATION, TO oppose hygiene (and become a partner, therefore, in the spread of disease), to burn witches, and even to incite people to war. When religion was hardly distinguishable from superstition, it was the accomplice on occasion of some of the worst evils which afflict mankind.

But teaching, medicine, surgery, and science have all been guilty in time past of harm. Sincere people have taught falsehoods, and the human body has been subjected to terrible treatment by physicians and surgeons who were working according to the best knowledge of their day. Eminent scientists have honestly announced "truths" which later turned out not to be truths at all, and have used their science in every generation in the service of war and death. We all have need to be humble when we think about our dogmatism in things which were wrong.

What Christians claim is, not that their past record is unblameable, and not that they have the answer to every question men could put, but that they have in Christ a self-disclosure of God, and that to follow him leads them into all the truth necessary for fullness of spiritual life. They claim this also: that although their understanding of the mind of God is slow, it is progressive; things that in one century they thought he would tolerate, they find with passing time he must condemn. So slavery went, and class and racial barriers are going—and the color bar and war will go as well.

Right at the heart of their faith is this compulsion to the best. Christians have much to regret in themselves and in their history, yet nothing but glory and gratitude for the One whose unworthy servants they are. He means, at the last, to perfect all who come to him. He knows where he is going and he has the whole wide world in his hands.

4

Can Religion Develop?

SOME PEOPLE ARE READY TO RECOGNIZE THAT UNDERSTANDING CAN grow in medicine, surgery, and science, but question whether that can apply to religion. If—as the old prophets and religious leaders claimed—God spoke to them . . . well, whatever God said should be for all time and beyond any need of "development."

But this ignores the difficulty of the human understanding of the divine mind. A man may see far more of God's will than anybody else living at the same time, and still not see all of it. The wisest, holiest man is remotely far from God. A God fully understood couldn't be God.

Not only are men slow to understand God's will; their obedience to it is slower still. People profess to hold a faith, but don't live up to it. Some are conscious hypocrites; more of them mean well but are weak. Hence it is easy for critics to point to these failures and sneer, "What a religion! There's nothing in it." One could as easily denounce the whole American police force because district officials have been guilty on occasion of taking bribes, or declare that the entire medical profession is corrupt because now and then a poor overworked doctor becomes a drug addict.

Religion—every religion—should be judged at its best. To refuse to face the challenge of the Sermon on the Mount because there was once a Spanish Inquisition, and people were burned for unbelief, is foolish. Christians know of their own past failures and repent them deeply. "Don't judge our faith by us," they say, "look at our best types and look at our Lord." Chesterton said of the Christian religion, "It hasn't been tried and found wanting. It has been found difficult and not really tried!"

5

Can the Existence of God Be Proved?

IT DEPENDS WHAT YOU MEAN BY PROOF. PROOF IS OF VARIOUS kinds. The proof most people prefer is scientific proof, where you can conduct exact experiments in exact conditions and obtain verification. But that kind of proof is possible only in a very limited area of life.

Mathematical proof is very satisfying in its own sphere. When the calculations confirm themselves in various ways, it leaves a sense of certainty which barely admits of doubt. But, again, that kind of proof is limited to its own world. In mathematics all the factors are really "given."

Logic has its own kind of proof. Granted the first statements on which the logical process proceeds, the thought can work through to an unquestionable conclusion. But many logical proofs get upset by a serious challenge to the first statements.

The major part of life is all outside the possibility of laboratory, mathematical, and logical proofs. Honor, justice, loyalty, or love (which are among the strongest forces in the universe) cannot be proved in any of these ways. Nor can you put God into a test tube.

Most life proceeds on enormous probabilities. Murder trials do. We hang men and say they were proved guilty, but none of the proof was of the kind listed above. Honest citizens can make mistakes in identifying people. Even solemn "confessions" have often proved false. Yet there is seldom any doubt at all that the verdict is true.

The arguments for the existence of God can't be worked out on a laboratory bench or by logic or maths; yet collectively they amount to an enormous probability, and if—on the probability—people will pray and experiment, they can have a personal certainty which allows them to say, "I know."

6

What Leads People to Believe in God?

THOUGHTFUL PEOPLE REALIZE THAT, IF THE EXISTENCE OF GOD cannot be proved on a laboratory bench or by mathematics or logic, neither can it be *dis*proved. The most learned and militant unbeliever has never been able to state the case against God so powerfully that belief was impossible. Deep thinkers have heard him out, weighed his arguments—and still believed in God. A vast number of leading scientists are among them.

The broad basis of their belief is, first, the existence of the world itself and the evidence of design in it. They know that some people say it "just happened," but they find that more fantastic than belief in a Creator. They could as easily believe that a truck driver dumped a heap of rubble by the River Thames and it turned into Westminster Abbey, as they could believe that this universe came into being without a vast mind behind it. Nor does belief in creation by evolving development rob them of the conviction that it had a Creator. "If this is true," they say, "it was clearly the method he used."

Secondly, they are impressed (as we have noticed already) by the fact that men and women everywhere have believed in God.

Unbelief is unnatural. Atheists have been known to pray in emergency.

Thirdly, they are aware of a moral sense within them. Every man and woman knows the word "ought," and not the word only, but the strong authoritative command of it. Nor is it clearly related (as some have said) to things which society has found convenient. We were born knowing that kindness is better than cruelty, the truth better than a lie, and that love is better than hate. Where did those certainties come from? How could we know them without being told? They are a thumbprint of the great hand that made us. The Creator is that *kind* of creator, and requires respect for those values in the creatures he has made.

7

How Do People Get Convinced About Religion?

THERE ARE MANY PRIVATE WAYS BY WHICH PEOPLE COME TO conviction in religion, though they are not our chief concern now. They may be convinced by the character of a real Christian, or the lovingkindness of a group of them. They might be privately brought to certainty about life after death, or witness some miraculous healing in response to prayer. But these are private reasons.

There are four chief ways to conviction in religion which can be explained and shared by all: The way of Authority, the way of Intuition, the way of Reason, the way of Experience. Before we look at each of them in turn, let me say something about them all.

They are not independent of each other. I went to Switzerland for my vacation last year. Three of my friends went too. We discovered our intentions by accident, and were amused at our different plans. One went by train through Paris and Vallorbe. One went by car through Burgundy to Geneva. Another went by bus through Brussels and Strasbourg to Basle. I flew from London to Zurich. Four ways which were quite independtent. We couldn't meet on the way.

It isn't like that with the four ways to conviction in religion; these ways intertwine. You can travel a bit on one and a bit on another. Serious seekers use all four. All branches of the Christian Church use all these ways, though they put them in different orders. Members of the Church of Rome put authority first. Quakers (who stress "the inner light") put intuition first. Methodists usually begin with experience. But *all use all*, because (at a deep level) all Christians belong to one another and are glad to share each others' insights.

Now let us look at each of these ways to conviction in turn.

8

Can You Be Convinced by Authority?

THE SHORTEST WAY TO BE SURE ABOUT ANYTHING IS TO ACCEPT it on high authority, and—if we deal specifically with the Christian religion—the highest authority is the Bible and the Church. Many people have come to satisfying conviction by the simple acceptance of the teaching of the Bible clearly interpreted in the living Church.

But the difficulty about this for other people is that, before you can have conviction this way, you must first accept the authority of the authority. How do they know that the Bible is dependable and the Church is its true interpreter?

Yet it is not irrational to accept things on high authority. If a surgeon says he must cut our body open and take something out, we let him. If a physician gives us medicine and says, "Take it three times a day," we take it—often without the slighest notion what it is. If a ship is in a violent storm at sea, no sane person suggests that the thousand passengers meet in the saloon and decide by majority vote how the ship should be handled; they trust the expert knowledge of the handful of officers and, in particular, of the captain himself. It isn't irrational to take things on authority; it is our daily habit. *We are careful in our selection of the authority*—we go to a highly qualified physician when we are ill and not to an African witch doctor—but we rely on authority.

"But isn't the Church itself divided," people say, "and don't scholars differ on Bible interpretation?" The Church is divided on some things, but increasing love is drawing the varied parts of it together, and the things on which they differ have been grossly exaggerated by their critics. There is only one *major* matter of conduct on which the Church is divided—whether or not Christians should go to war. On nearly every really important moral question the Church speaks with one voice.

There is authority here—high authority. People who are not themselves experts in theology and Bible interpretation should bear in mind that the way of Authority is still a way worthy of respect.

9

Can You Be Convinced by Intuition?

THERE ARE SOME THINGS WE KNOW WITHOUT BEING TOLD. WE didn't read them in a book. They didn't have to be knocked into us by our teachers. No scientific experiment was necessary to prove them. We just *know* them.

We always know (as we have already noted) that love is better than hate and kindness better than cruelty.

We always know that beauty pulls us. People vary in the way they respond to beauty, but all feel it—in a flower, in a landscape, in a sunset, in a symphony. It needs no justification; its proof is in itself.

We always know that truth is better than a lie—however convenient lying might be on occasion! Nor is it truth only in the conversation of day to day—but truth in its deepest sense—the truth of things. What a thrill to solve a problem and find the *truth!*

We always know that goodness is better than badness—even if it appeals to us more in some lovely deed of sacrifice than in strict obedience to a high moral code. Who can be unmoved by the goodness of Elizabeth Pilenko, the Russian nun who, on Good Friday, 1945, saw a hysterical girl in the line for the gas chamber at Ravensbruck Concentration Camp and said, "Don't be frightened. Look, I'll take your turn . . . ," and went to death in her place?

Beauty, truth, goodness—how real and high they are! Even when we spurn them, we know in ourselves that we are spurning the best. How do we know? We just do! They are inside us. Animals don't feel like this. We have sight and *insight*.

If we follow these insights, they lead us to a Being to whom beauty, truth, and goodness are supremely precious. Thus the way of Intuition also is a way worthy of respect.

10

Can You Be Convinced by Reason?

SOME PEOPLE ALMOST RESENT THE WAY OF AUTHORITY AND TEND to reject anything that they are taught. So far from believing that their teachers are seeking to pass on to them the best our race has learned in every area of life, they half suspect that the teachers are trying to impose outmoded ideas on them in order to preserve the present order of things. But a thing isn't wrong because it is taught. I began arithmetic by learning that one and one make two, and I have had no reason in all the intervening years to doubt it.

These people may sincerely doubt the adequacy, also, of the way of Intuition. "It could *confirm* things," a man said to me once, "if I had been convinced of them by any other means." To all such, the way of Reason offers a road ahead—a long, difficult, and sometimes circuitous one, but those who persist in it may hope to come to conviction, though not to certainty; and the little leap of faith (as we shall show later) can bring them even there.

We are, in a sense, on the way of Reason in this book. We are facing difficult questions. We are beginning with life where we meet it, rather than with the body of doctrine the Church could offer to us. We are trying honestly to clear the ground by our own thought to see whether we could venture here in trust, or experiment there, say, in prayer. We know enough already to know that God cannot be *dis*proved, and perhaps the hope is already in us that his existence and nature can be put beyond all reasonable doubt.

Let us press on. This is not the most crowded way to our goal, though almost all people use it on part of the journey. We saw that those who travel mainly by the way of Authority use reason in selecting the authority they follow. But to some, this must be the *main* way, and on this route one can travel to conviction with G. J. Romanes, and C. E. M. Joad, and C. S. Lewis (to name only three out of hundreds of thousands).

11

Can You Be Convinced by Experience?

THE FOURTH WAY TO CONVICTION IS THE WAY OF EXPERIENCE. It is the claim to know God personally—not just to know things *about* him, but to know *him*. If I may intrude with a personal witness, I myself make that claim. I do not see visions, or hear external voices, but I know what it is to be in the presence of God, and to have the evil in me beaten down and the good built up.

But all this is very *private*. One can tell of these things, but not give them to another. Many sincere unbelievers say that it is all delusion and how can we prove that it isn't. I would ask them to consider these points:

Millions have this experience. This claim is not made by a handful of peculiar people. Millions have claimed it through the ages; millions claim it still. They are not mental cases, or drawn from one class or intelligence group. They are of *all* kinds.

They include some of the greatest benefactors of our race. Even people who think religious experience is a delusion admit the amazing lives and service of those who claim it. All the high religions have such people, but perhaps the great army of Christian saints is unsurpassed in the history of our race. Some were changed from appalling wickedness by their experience. If all this is the fruit of delusion, then delusion is more wonderful than sanity!

Their reports coincide. If religious experience is private delusion, we should not expect what these people say to coincide, but—in all the main parts of their witness—they *do*. They have fellowship with Another—wise, loving, and bent upon goodness, truth, and beauty. Is all this to be pushed aside as the dreams of "crackpots," or the invention of "half-baked revivalists"?

If you have no experience of it yourself, are you not driven to believe, either that millions of other people are nitwits (or liars) , or that they *do* have the experience they claim?

Well, those are the four chief ways to conviction. Remember that you are not confined to one of them. They intertwine and confirm each other.

Where do we go from here?

12

How Does a Man Move from Conviction to Certainty?

WHAT CAN AN OPEN-MINDED MAN DO IN THIS BEWILDERING WORLD, if he sincerely wants to find God for himself? He may not yet be convinced that God is there—but if he hasn't closed his mind on the point and firmly decided that God is *not* there, how can he put it to the test?

He must make an experiment. The only way to be quite sure is to act as if God is there and then you will *know* he is. Don't be put off by the condition! It is the only way to knowledge in many areas of life. There are lots of things you will never know unless you take what seems a risk to find out. Act as though it is true and you will know that it is.

It is like swimming. If a man decided that he would never go into the water until he knew how to swim, he would never swim. The venture is part of the knowing. It is against all "common sense" that, if you lay a human body on the sea, the sea will hold it up. Yet it does. You can never know until you prove it yourself. Other people can tell you and show you, but you can never be sure until you do something which feels risky (if not mad), until you get into the water and take your feet off the bottom.

Even then, you will need patience and help—perhaps a lot of patience and help. But, if you persist, you will swim. You will know—as I have known these many years—the delight of thrashing through the water and finding the water holding you up.

We call this initial venture "faith" (or, at least, the beginning of it), and because some people think that there is a catch in it somewhere, we ought to look a little more closely at it.

13

What Is Faith?

FAITH IS THIS KIND OF TRUST WE HAVE JUST DESCRIBED. SOME people think that it is peculiar to religion and that it is putting blinkers on your eyes.

Faith is not peculiar to religion. It is found all through life. We use faith when we get on a bus. (There are accidents every week.) We use faith when we go into a restaurant to eat. (People have got food poisoning before now.) We use faith when we send our children to school. (The teachers may put terrible fears into their little minds.) We use a lot of faith when we get married. (Think of the awful number of divorces!) Faith . . . faith . . . faith! All life is lived by faith. It should not surprise us that we meet the need for faith in religion.

Here is the plain fact. As with the swimming, you can't be sure without it. The Bible is quite frank on the point. It says: "He that cometh to God must believe that he is, and that he is a rewarder of them that diligently seek him." (Heb. 11:6.) Christ said, "If any man will do his will, he shall know of the doctrine." (John 7:17.) It is not "know and do" (as we should like it), but "do and know"—as with the swimming and so much else in life.

Well, why not get into the water? Only experiment can issue in experience. If you really want to be sure, put this thing to the test. Pray. Talk to God, believing that he will hear you. Read the Bible; it has fed the lives of multimillions through nearly two thousand years and could feed your life too. Put yourself into fellowship with a group of vital Christians.

14

Are All Christians Certain?

No. THOUGH MANY CHRISTIANS HAVE A SENSE OF COMPLETE assurance in their religion, others frankly feel that they have never yet got beyond a place of honest trust.

They have looked at life with all its strange contradictions and have definitely decided that the Christian position (despite its difficulties) makes more sense of the world than any of the other explanations which have been offered, and they have boldly ventured themselves on it. Yet they could not truly say that they have passed the point where doubts cease to recur, and there are times and circumstances when they find themselves going over the arguments again.

But these occasions grow less frequent as they travel. The circumstances recur, but not the doubts—or not with their old power. The more they seek to live with Christ in their thought, the more sure do they become of his reality and help; and there are times when the assurance which others seem always to enjoy comes flooding in on them, and they wonder how they could ever doubt again.

And, despite these periods of doubt, these men and women are Christians. They are not relying on their own grasp of things, but on Christ. They are walking (even if they stumble now and then) in his way. They believe it to be completely rational, when one is faced with a dilemma, to press forward on the more promising path; and the merit of this path (they find) is that it is strangely self-authenticating, and the farther they go the more sure do they become.

But perhaps there are other things which may make a man hesitate before he makes this venture, and at which we ought now to look.

15

Couldn't All Religion Be Wishful Thinking?

THERE ARE PEOPLE WHO HESITATE TO EMBARK ON THE ADVENTURE of faith because they think that all religion may be wishful thinking. Men cannot face the idea of a godless, meaningless universe (they suspect), and they invent a supreme and kindly Being behind things. But he may be only the fruit of their fears and wishes and have no basis in reality at all.

Let us look at that possibility. The world itself is not the fruit of wishful thinking. Geology has taught us nothing if it has not taught us that the world was here long before man came to "think" it. Man, as we know him, is a late arrival on this planet. And if the world, and the evidence of design in it, is part of the reason for believing in God, that is clearly not the fruit of wishful thinking.

Nor is the moral sense in man. People who believe that all religious experience is a delusion sometimes say that folk who think that they listen to God speaking inside them always hear what they want to hear.

It isn't true. The animal in man might think that he had a right to any woman he could persuade, but the God he meets within him withstands his wild appetites and requires that he be loyal to his mate. The coward and schemer in man often thinks that a lie is not only convenient but permissible, yet the God he meets inside him insists on the truth, whatever the personal cost.

Wishful thinking? No doubt there *is* such a thing, and we have all been guilty on occasion of half-believing something to be true because we *wanted* to believe it. But that cannot explain religion. The God who confronts us in our conscience with moral commandments which run directly opposite to our lusting desires isn't a figment of our wishful thinking. He is the great Other, whom someday we must all meet.

16

Isn't Life Easier if You Are an Atheist?

IT IS, IN SOME WAYS. RULES ARE ALWAYS AWKWARD THINGS TO our selfish human nature and it is nice to believe that there aren't any absolute ones. Conscience is an annoying murmur inside any man of strong passions who has a firm determination to get what he wants, so it is easier to brush the silly things aside if you can convince yourself that it is just the generalization of social custom and has no real authority.

There are other advantages in being an atheist. The problem of pain and suffering, which is a near-nightmare to people who believe in a God of love, is no problem to him at all. The charge of hypocrisy (which is constantly leveled at Christians if they stumble in their highway) can never be brought against him. Indeed, he can get an extra glow of virtue when he does a good turn, because he is under no supernatural constraint to live a life of love. He can say to his companions at work, "Look at me. I believe in nothing, but I'm always doing good turns." It is nice to remember, after all this, that many atheists are not like the people depicted above, but (benefiting often by the moral fruit of the religion they have discarded) they are kind, unselfish, humble people, and good colleagues in the fight against social evils.

But are there any important losses to set down beside the "gains" the atheist appears to enjoy? There are. We must look at most of them more fully later, but some of them can be mentioned here.

He must give up all hope of finding any deep meaning in life. If he himself loves beauty, truth, and goodness, his own love of them are inexplicable and their origin a complete mystery. Did matter alone produce beauty, truth, goodness, and his own deep care for them? All noble men, sacrificing themselves for their ideals, are an enigma; Jesus Christ (whom the atheist can classify only as a man) is the greatest enigma of all. When the atheist is grateful, he has no one to thank. He has no hope of reunion with his dear ones beyond the grave. He misses the companionship of God in this life (life's greatest treasure, as Christians think) and may get so firmly fixed on the path which leads to outer darkness that he will miss the best in the next life as well.

17

Isn't It Best to Be Agnostic?

AN AGNOSTIC IS NOT AN ATHEIST. HE DOESN'T SAY THERE ISN'T A God. He says, "I don't know. Perhaps there is; perhaps there isn't. Who can tell?" Many agnostics feel strongly that their position is rational and humble and as far as they can go.

We recognize and respect this position. We have conceded that God cannot be proved by a scientific experiment, by mathematics, or by irresistible logic. We have shown that the only way to personal certainty is by an act of faith which the agnostic (even if he is a swimmer!) will not take.

Is there, then, no way forward? Must his loyalty to fixed ideas of how truth should be understood remain forever a barrier to truth itself? Is he to be left saying, "I have no personal experience of God, and the arguments for his existence break even. There is love in the world—but hate also. There is design in the world—but chaos too. *I don't know.* Beyond this no man of mental integrity can go!"

Can't he? Not one step more? Isn't it true that when an honest mind faces an even argument, and life itself presses for a decision, with no loss of integrity, a man should back the higher alternative, and his own sensitive conscience will approve him in what he does?

For those are the facts. When the road forks, a man can mark time all his life at the fork (which is what the agnostic does), or take one of the two ways. He can decide that this as a pur-

poseless universe and "build his house on the rock of unyielding despair" (as one traveler on this path describes it) , or make
the experiment of faith which *could* issue in the discovery of
understanding, meaning, purpose, peace, joy. Is it so unscientific
to experiment? Why not take the path which makes sense?

And—remember this—even Christians are agnostic about
many things. They don't claim to have "all the answers."

18

Are There Two Kinds of Agnostic?

YES, THERE ARE. THERE ARE THOSE (WHOM WE HAVE JUST BEEN
considering) who deny that God is knowable; but there are
others who say that, while he may be knowable, he isn't known
to them.

The distinction is important and deep. If you are an agnostic,
you ought to be clear, first, what kind of agnostic you are.

To say quite definitely that God can't be known is a bold
affirmation. It seems tantamount to saying that "what I don't
know can't be known." It appears to label the saints and seers
and prophets of all the ages (whose insights are among the
treasures of our race) as sadly misguided men.

A little girl came home from school one day and announced
triumphantly, "I know all the tables; even twelve times twelve."
Her grandpa said, with a twinkle in his eye, "What is thirteen
times thirteen?" and the little girl answered with instant scorn,
"Don't be silly, Grandpa. There is no such thing."

We can forgive finality in a little girl, but no rational man
would claim that the limits of his knowledge were the limits of
all knowledge; that because he didn't know a thing, nobody
else did.

What about the other kind of agnostic—the man who admits that God *may* be knowable but isn't known to *him?*

To that man we can say only, "How much time are you prepared to give to learn what God is like? Do you admit that the Creator (if he is there) has claims on you? If you would willingly give months and months to learn a foreign language, would you be willing to give as much time to learn about God?"

Frankly, this high quest is not just for scamped moments. God has said, "Ye shall seek me, and find me, *when ye shall search for me with all your heart.*" (Jer. 29:13.)

19

Can Men Know God?

WE HAVE ADMITTED THAT RELIGIOUS EXPERIENCE IS PERSONAL, and that one man can't give it to another. The fact that millions have it, that it produces the finest quality of character, and that the experiences of devout men correspond on all major points, has been offered as evidence that this isn't the private delusion of the mentally unbalanced or just waves of emotion. But is there more that can be said about the nature of Christian experience?

Men to whom religion is life know themselves to be in touch with someone else. The more attention they give to God, the more they are aware of it. There are, of course, thousands of people who profess a high religion and do nothing about it, and they may have less experience of God than an agnostic who feels haunted by the God he can't accept. But the devout *know.* They may be deep philosophers or simple peasants, but their experience is the same.

They find the center of their life moved from self to God.

With the years, they are delivered from the obsession with self which is set so deeply in our human nature. It ceases to be natural to them to think, "I . . . I . . . I . . ." and "Me . . . Me . . . Me . . . ." They sense a sublime purpose behind all things. Their own little life is caught up in big issues, and they often feel upon them the pressure of a higher hand.

Unexpected light falls for them on the mysteries of life. When they cannot explain why dark things happen, they are still serene, because they are sure that the God behind all things is deeply wise and deeply loving. They stand up to the severe testings of life with courage and confidence. When the doctor shakes his head over them, when they feel a grim disease creeping up their body, when a dear one is certified insane, when their dearest has inoperable cancer, when the coffin is standing beside the bed—they are never more sure of the nearness of God.

"Delusion . . . delusion" chants the militant unbeliever. "Nothing in it. All delusion."

How does he know? And whom would you rather live with—someone who denies all deep meaning to life and is (at the best) stoical in the face of great suffering, or someone who, out of suffering, can speak a sure word about God?

20

Could It Be That I Don't Want to Believe?

IT COULD. SOME PEOPLE OPPOSE RELIGION FOR PURELY PRIVATE reasons. There are even people irrational enough to deny the existence of God and then rail at the God who (they say) isn't there. But anybody who is bitter about religion deserves understanding and tenderness.

Many who seem to hate God have had a hard life and have suffered terrible hurts. Some, malformed at birth, have dragged their way through life, scorning all talk of providence. Some lost a mother in childhood, or life's partner soon after being married. Some are disfigured, unloved, maladjusted. They have won no inner victory over the buffetings of life. All deserve patience, sympathy, and understanding. Moreover, we must face those awful problems later in this book.

Some who scorn religion were given a poor impression of it in childhood. Some have been let down by church people (or think they have), and have transferred their dislike to the church, or to God himself. One bitter man with whom I once talked loathed all parsons because his boy had been corrupted by a sex pervert in holy orders. His bitterness was understandable, but—as he came to see—unintelligent. He hadn't lost faith in all bank managers because a rare one is a rogue. God is there, and God is good, whatever the parsons are.

Some people shrink from religion because they don't want to get "involved." They fear the sacrifices it may entail. Some don't want to believe because of sin in their own lives. Their anxiety to disprove the existence of God, and life after death, is not the pure passion for truth. Unbelief, as well as belief, can spring from the heart as well as the mind. A man resolutely breaking the commandments, and bothered by a conscience which won't keep quiet, often looks for "reasons" to disbelieve in God.

If you really don't *want* to believe in religion, you ought to examine your mind on the point. Why this exuberance when God is disposed of? Is it sane to have a party to celebrate the death of your dearest hopes? Could there be some other reason why you are glad?

21

Can't I Be Moral Without Religion?

OF COURSE YOU CAN! MANY PEOPLE ARE. MILLIONS OF PEOPLE
who appear to ignore God are kind, neighborly, good citizens.
and admirable members of society. Does it matter that religion
means nothing to them?

Some of these people have more religion than appears on the
surface. They may never go to church, but they have some faith
in God, and pray in great need. They have had their babies
baptized, and it wasn't pure superstition; they honestly wanted
the blessing of God on the little one. They were married in
church and not in a Justice of the Peace office. They have a
dim idea that the great and good God rules over all things. A
funeral without some kind of religious service is almost unknown.

These people ought to come closer into religion. They need
(as all men need) to be *sure* of God. If religion isn't honestly
practiced, it has less and less effect on our private lives and on
the community. One of the reasons for the moral decline of our
nation is the neglect of sound religion. Moreover, sooner or
later in life, great troubles come to us all. Unless we keep close
to God, he isn't able to help us in our need in the way his love
desires.

In addition to all these people who have more religion than
one might suppose, there is a very much smaller number who
flatly deny the existence of God, and many of them are highly
moral too. They are quite sure that one can have morals without religion, and there is no sound reason for denying that.

Nonetheless, it is beyond serious question that vital religion
is a great buttress to morality. If a man under strong temptation
thinks the moral rules are just a human invention, he will be

40

less likely to keep them than a man who deeply believes that God gave the Ten Commandments and is the supreme upholder of the moral order. That is why anyone who feels sure that he can keep the moral code without divine help ought to ask himself whether his children and grandchildren will be able to do so too.

22

What Would I Lose, if I Shut Religion Out?

ALMOST EVERYTHING WHICH GIVES PRECIOUSNESS AND MEANING TO life.

Some people dispute that. "Without religion," they say, "you still have life, love, flowers, music—and lots of other wonderful things. Enjoy them and be thankful."

Yes, but a doom hangs over them all. Nothing in this life stays. Death parts the most loyal lovers, flowers fade, the music dies on the ear. Without religion there is no sense in things. Did you watch your own dear child die? Do you remember the look in her eyes? "So what? Put the body in the earth. There's no sense in things."

No, but there's infinite sadness in them. Don't pretend that life on those terms *satisfies* you. An eminent unbeliever (as we have already noted) says that the most you can achieve on this road is "unyielding despair." Don't try to deceive yourself that you like it that way. It's religion or the dark.

Other things gnaw at you too. What of the awful injustices of life—the blind, and lame, and maimed, and mad? Are they just unlucky?

It is foolish to say (as some do) that all questions about "the meaning of life" are "meaningless." People will go on seeking

41

meaning, however much clever people tell them that they've "got the words wrong." Every uncomplicated man wants to make sense of things, and deep in his mind is the belief that there *is* sense in life somewhere.

Religion is seeking the sense. It does not claim to clear up all mysteries, but it claims to have the clue to meaning. It believes that it can convince men by reason alone that the way of prayer and worship should be tried; and it claims, also, that those who follow the clue with determination will make personal discoveries and come to assurance.

Nothing else in life even offers the hope. If you are sincere in saying that you have had all of life you want, what a poor life you've had!

23

Isn't It Something That I'm Interested in Religion?

IT ISN'T REALLY. PEOPLE CAN BE INTERESTED IN ANYTHING— earthworms, darts, bebop, mesmerism, and (as we mentioned before) stamp collecting. Religion doesn't go into this category. Apart from other things, being interested in religion is worlds away from having it. Indeed, the people who have religion never talk that way. They don't "have religion"; they have God.

Just being interested in religion costs you nothing in money, effort, discipline—and next to nothing in time. It never interferes with Sunday morning golf, or lying in bed, or any other pleasures. You can just read a book on it when the fancy takes you, or argue about it with a pal, but it never really *costs* anything.

That wouldn't matter if it got you anywhere. But it doesn't.

People can be "interested" in religion all their lives and be never an inch nearer God. A sincere atheist is more likely to get religion than most of the people who are merely "interested" in it. He is honestly aware of its importance. He deeply feels that "God or no God?" is the major question of the universe. Don't deceive yourself that being interested in religion is something in your favor. The chances are that you are using this cheap and mild interest to evade the God who is seeking you all the time, and who would find you if you would give up these evasive tactics.

There is only one way to personal certainty about these things. It is commital. You must—as we have argued—make the venture. Pray. Learn to worship. Study the Bible. Seek friendship with people who know God for themselves.

It comes back to the swimming illustration again. You can be interested in swimming all your life and never swim.

Jump in.

24

Is Religion a Kind of Gamble?

IN A WAY, YES. IF A MAN HAS HAD NO RELIGIOUS INSTRUCTION IN childhood (or has forgotten what he had) and comes to think freshly about religion with a mature mind, he often feels that the first serious beginning is a gamble. He won't think so later on. When he comes to religious conviction from his own awareness of God, nothing will seem *less* like a gamble, but at the beginning it is a bit like stepping into the dark.

Life is in some ways so contradictory. What are we to make of earthquakes, famines, and floods? Why does one set of animals feed on another? Isn't the diphtheria germ part of creation too? Yet there is mother love all through nature, and wonderful evidence of willing sacrifice. Flowers and sunsets are both beautiful, and if there *is* a Being behind creation, it is hard to think that the One who shaped the flower and painted the sunset is unkind.

If we turn from the contradictions of nature to listen to the opinions of scholars, there is more contradiction. Clearly science and unbelief don't necessarily go together. Many of the most eminent scientists are completely convinced of the truths of religion, though others equally eminent are unbelievers. It is no good firing off one big name against another. Religion is a very private thing in some ways. At the last, a man must make up his mind for himself.

The argument of this book is that a man should do the bold and hopeful thing. The reasons for it are *at least* as strong as those against it—many would say "much stronger." Back the higher alternative. Gamble on the larger hope. Act (as we have said before) as though God is there, and you will find that he is. Pray. Give time to the Bible (though under direction if possible and with some explanations). Join in worship. Any church will welcome you. The communion you were brought up in might be the best, or you could go with a Christian friend to *his* church.

But make the venture. The finest things of earth and heaven are within your grasp.

25

Where Do We Go from Here?

MAYBE WE HAVE GONE AS FAR AS WE CAN, WITHIN THE LIMITS OF this little book, on religion in general. Most of the things we have said until now would apply to all the "world religions." It is time to examine the special claims of the Christian faith.

It is a basic conviction in the Christian Church that God has visited this planet in person. Some people find the idea quite shocking. "If there is a great God behind this universe," they argue, "let him remain great. He must be (if he exists) all but beyond the reach of human thought. To suggest that God could be born, and seen, and touched, is insulting to the intelligence, and drags man's highest ideas to the earth."

Yet this is what Christians believe. They understand the offensiveness of the idea to some minds, but they affirm that *it happened*. Nor does the idea seem shocking to them—but wonderful. They reason like this: if God is there, if God has a special love for men and women, if the end of creation (through a vast unfolding process) is to bring men and women into the closest relationship to God, why should it seem offensive that God should come to earth himself? If, indeed, fellowship with human beings was his purpose, was he not compelled to give some such revelation? The vast mathematical order of the universe reveals something of his mind; flowers and sunsets may disclose his love of beauty; but only a person can reveal a person. If man was to know God in any fullness, wasn't God under constraint to show himself more intimately than nature could ever reveal him?

So Christians believe. God, they say, who is behind all history, entered history himself in the person of Jesus Christ. He was born, lived an earthly life, died, and showed himself after death living still.

It is time to consider the revelation of God in Jesus Christ.

45

26
What Do We Know of Jesus Christ?

HE WAS BORN 6 B.C., OF A YOUNG WOMAN NOT MARRIED, IN AN out-of-the-way place called Bethlehem. He grew up in an unsanitary village named Nazareth. With no known distinction of birth, belonging to a despised people, denied the best education of his day and race, he was trained as a carpenter. At about thirty years of age, he laid aside the tools of his trade and began to teach and preach and heal. Although the common people heard him gladly, he never touched world affairs in any obvious way. His whole life was lived in one obscure province of the Roman Empire, and his travels were limited to an area half the size of New Jersey. After three years of ministry he was arrested on suspicion of leading a popular revolt, and was executed by crucifixion. The life which began in shadowed obscurity ended in public shame. But not *very* public. The whole matter seemed beneath the interest of "people of quality," and his name was so unimportant that it wasn't even mentioned in any official document which has ever come to light.

Two thousand years have now passed by. Nearly a third of the world worships him. It is a safe guess to say that another third holds him (as Mr. Gandhi did) in enormous respect. He has inspired the mightiest music and the greatest art the world has known. People have died for him in every generation since he himself suffered. Multitudes would die for him today. Indeed, some who deny belief in all religion consider that his rule of love would save the world.

46

Who was this strange peerless person? The Christian Church is built on a conviction that he was God himself.

27

How Could God Become Man?

CHRISTIANS BELIEVE, AS FIRMLY AS THE OLD HEBREWS BELIEVED, that there is one great God over all—but they believe that there is society in the Godhead. In the oneness of God there are united (they say) three Persons: the Father, the Son, and the Holy Spirit. (An eminent Jewish rabbi once told me in private—and as a simple illustration—that he did not find this teaching difficult to understand. It reminded him of the flame of a candle —one light, but three colors clearly in it.)

It was God the Son who, at the Father's desire and by his own willingness, came to earth as a man. The Bible says he "emptied himself, taking the form of a servant" (Phil. 2:7 R.S.V.). As far as humanity can disclose deity, he revealed the life of God to men.

Christians freely admit their inability fully to understand, or completely to explain, how Christ could be both man and God, but to that double assertion they have held on with unshakeable assurance through the centuries. They have come to regard Jesus, not only as a messenger, but—in an sense—as himself the message.

In Christ, many of the things expressed by wise men in the past concerning God received their confirmation. God is holy, and calls for purity in men and women. He is loving, and his best human name is "Father." He tries to win love from his human children, and patiently seeks those who have turned

47

from his ways. He gladly forgives all who are sorry for their wrongdoing and who turn to him in penitence.

Yet it is not only what Jesus *said* that means much to Christians; they are moved even more by what he *was*. Compassion ruled all he did. When he was angry, it was at injuries done not to himself but to others. When he spoke with terrible sternness to the religious leaders of his day, it was love that made him angry. The religious leaders were giving the poor people the wrong picture of God, and Jesus was angry through love for the misguided poor. Jesus feared for these leaders who had called the light "darkness" so often that they had come to believe it themselves.

28

Do We Know Enough About Jesus Christ?

SOME PEOPLE HESITATE TO ACCEPT THE BELIEF THAT CHRIST WAS God on earth on the ground that we do not know enough to form a judgment.

The Bible includes four very brief biographies of Jesus. Indeed, they are too brief to be called "biographies" in any robust sense; they were selections from what the writers had seen or heard. Three of them use a good deal of the same material, and all of them give most of their attention to the last days of his life. "Is that enough," these people ask, "to serve as the basis for so immense a claim?"

The material is scanty (as Christians readily allow), but the picture which emerges is clear, compelling, and above the level of the writers' imaginations. Christ's teaching (which fulfills the noblest hopes of the Jewish people among whom he was born) is sublime, and the picture of his person is one beyond the invention of the Galilean fishermen who set it down. Indeed, though they had divine assistance in making their record, they were men working with human words, and they must have felt themselves how inadequate the best words were to report the glory which had been revealed. In some ways, the wonder is not that we do not know more, but that we know so much.

Yet it is not on the biographies alone that we depend for our belief about Jesus Christ. His effect on the people who followed him is part of the evidence too. These men were Jews, and firm in their high conviction of the unity of God, yet *they* came to believe that the man they had lived with was too big for any human category, and that in him an ancient promise had been fulfilled and God had visited and redeemed his people. They were the first to believe it, but nearly one in three in the world believes it now.

29

Couldn't Christ Have Been Just a Good Man?

IT IS EASIER IN SOME WAYS TO BELIEVE THAT CHRIST WAS AN impostor or mad than to believe that he was just a good man.

He made such immense claims for himself. He said, "The Son of man is Lord of the sabbath" (Luke 6:5); "I am the way, the truth, and the life" (John 14:6); "He that hath seen me hath seen the Father" (John 14:9); "Whosoever shall lose his life for my sake . . . shall save it" (Mark 8:35).

He forgave sins. He said, "Be of good cheer; thy sins be forgiven" (Matt. 9:2); "Her sins, which are many, are forgiven" (Luke 7:47); "The Son of man hath power upon earth to forgive sins" (Luke 5:24); "Neither do I condemn thee: go, and sin no more" (John 8:11). The bystanders saw the point

49

of all this and asked in bewilderment, "Who can forgive sins, but God alone?" (Luke 5:21).

He had no sense of sin himself. Every good man has a sense of sin. The better the man, the keener his sense of sin. But Christ had no sense of sin. He said one day to his accusers, "Which of you convicts me of sin?" (John 8:46 R.S.V.)

He accepted worship. Worship belongs only to God. Any good man would be appalled at being worshiped. Christ accepted worship. "They that were in the boat worshiped him" (Matt. 14:33 R.S.V.), "They came and took hold of his feet and worshiped him" (Matt. 28:9 R.S.V.), "And he worshiped him" (John 9:38 R.S.V.).

Add all this up. It still leaves aside the dependability of the Bible record, to which we must turn later, and there are texts to set beside these in which he seems deliberately to hide his deity; but let it be said now, that with the evidence before them, Christians have felt driven to choose between three possibilites: that he was an impostor, quite mad—or God. For nearly two thousand years they have made answer: "Very God of very God."

30

Did Christ Live a Perfect Life?

YES, BUT BE CAREFUL TO UNDERSTAND THE SENSE OF THE WORD "perfect." A completely perfect life could be lived only in a perfect world, and Christ came to live in *this* world—a wicked, in some ways hateful, world. If he had been living in a perfect world, there would have been no turning out of the traders from the Temple (Mark 11:15-18), no criticism of the Pharisees (Matt. 23), and no talk of hell (Matt. 5:21-32). When Christians say that Christ lived a perfect life, they mean that he always acted from a perfect motive.

The people who deny that Christ lived a perfect life usually do it on three grounds—his sharp attack on the priests, scribes, and Pharisees; his terrible words about hell; his withering of the fig tree (Matt. 21:18-22). Most critics admit themselves that these things are "odd," and do not fit into the whole lovely picture of him. Let us look at each of them in turn.

He attacked the priests, scribes, and Pharisees. Some people say that he told us to be loving, but he wasn't very loving to them. Love is sometimes terribly stern. I had a most loving mother. She was wise too. She said things (on occasion) to me, the memory of which makes me wince after nearly fifty years; but they were all motivated by love. I could have gone wrong, but her blistering words saved me.

Hell is real and we must refer to that later. It is best defined as separation from God, and some of the lurid language Jesus used was metaphorical. To see people he deeply cared for turning their back on God, and deliberately walking into the outer darkness moved him to the most awful warnings. And again the motive was love.

The withering of the fig tree is an incident apart. At a cursory reading, it looks as if Christ was petulant for a moment; but deeper scrutiny banishes the thought. He was teaching his disciples an enormously important lesson about faith. It was worth sacrificing a tree to fix it in their minds.

He lived a perfect life in the sense that he acted always from a perfect motive.

31

Did Christ Work Miracles?

YES, HE DID. BUT WE MUST BE CAREFUL WHAT WE MEAN BY A miracle. A miracle, in the New Testament, is an event outside the understood chain of cause and effect. Some people have found the miracles of the Bible an obstacle to belief because they think the universe runs (and must run) on unchanging laws of causation, and that, even if God himself were to interfere with them, life would be chaos.

While this is true, it must be remembered that men themselves have discovered in God's universe higher laws and still higher laws, and, working one with another, have done things their fathers would have called "miracles." It is a law of the universe that iron will not float, but great liners shuttle across the Atlantic. It is a law of the universe that steel will not hang in the air, but mighty airplanes are leaping over all the oceans and continents of the world. No laws are broken, but one law is woven with another. If *men* can do this with their limited knowledge of the universe, what can *God* do who made all things? And if Christ were God on earth, would you not *expect* him to have powers above the ordinary?

It may be that the miracles of Christ were performed by the use of laws at present unknown to men, but the important thing to notice is their character. They weren't "tricks" or "magic." He never used miracles just to impress people ("Have you seen this one?"). With the exception of the withering of the fig tree (which we have glanced at already) they were works of mercy and love. They were the kind of things you would expect God to do, if God visited this earth. Compassion, tenderness, and pity lie behind them all.

Notice this also: Christ never used these supernatural powers for himself—never turned stones into bread when he was hungry, and refused to step down from the cross when they nailed him there.

32

Did Christ Know Everything?

NO. THE BIBLE SAYS (AS WE HAVE NOTED) THAT WHEN CHRIST came to our world he "emptied himself, taking the form of a servant" (Phil. 2:7). He didn't descend to earth in a chariot of fire. He entered life, as we do, from a woman's womb.

We cannot hope to pierce the mystery of his self-consciousness. When did he know who he was? Not as a baby lying in the manger. We have but one glimpse of him in childhood, where he appears as a boy who was very much in love with God's house, and was what people today would call "very precocious." How he grew to realize his unique relationship to his Father above, and the special character of his mission on earth, we can only guess, but he knew it long before he left his bench and was baptized. He strode out into public life saying, "The kingdom of heaven is at hand."

Yet he still had the form of a servant and he was still subject to many of the limitations of humanity. He was disappointed with people on some occasions—and surprised on others. There were things he did not know, and he said so (Mark 13:32). He wrestled with himself, before he went to his death, until he was in a bloody sweat.

Yet he was utterly plain, and completely authoritative, and satisfyingly comprehensive on all the things which men most need to know. He really knew the Father above. Life has meaning, he said. God is over all. He is holy, loving, and merciful.

He meets penitence with pardon and enjoys forgiving. Yet he *will* have righteousness, and those who deliberately spurn him come under awful condemnation.

Christ knew everything we most need to know.

33

Did Christ Rise from the Dead?

CHRISTIANS ARE COMPLETELY CONVINCED THAT HE DID. IF IT IS said that nobody else ever did, it can be said also that nobody else has influenced the world as he has done. If he was unique in life, is it a thing incredible that he should be unique in his way of leaving it?

Something astonishing happened to found the Christian Church. To suppose that a bunch of Galilean fishermen did it without some amazing event is harder to believe than the miracle itself. Nor was it a tale which slowly grew with the years. It was being told three days after his death, and publicly and effectively preached within eight weeks.

No rival theory has withstood careful examination. It has been said by some (against all the evidence) that he wasn't dead when they took him from the Cross, and by others that his friends stole the body away. But can you really believe that? If you do, you will also have to believe that his disciples spent the rest of their lives preaching a lie they had invented themselves, and that finally they were prepared to be executed for it.

Some have said that it was all hallucination. But hallucination normally turns on expectation—and they were *not* expecting it. Thomas was as "hardheaded" as a man could be. He wouldn't believe when his ten closest friends swore to him before God that it was true. Then he saw Christ himself. Hallucination can account for some queer things, but not this. So *many* saw him—on one occasion, five hundred at once.

This thing happened. Christians are not arguing in a circle, asking men to believe that Christ was God on earth because he returned from the dead, and to believe then that he returned from the dead because he was God. Think of the quality of his life; think of his impact on all subsequent history; think what he does still with men and women if they only give him a chance. It is of this unique person that we are speaking.

Part of his mission on earth was to show men and women that death is not a blind alley but a highway to life.

He came back from the dead to prove it.

34

Why Is Christ Called "Saviour"?

MAN IS LOST. THE FACT THAT HE DOESN'T REALIZE IT DOESN'T mean that it isn't true. A policeman who saw a little boy crying in the street and said "Are you lost, Sonny?," received the tearful reply, "No, *I'm* not lost. Mummy's lost." But he *was* lost. His anxious mother knew where *she* was, and she knew the way home. It was the little boy who was lost.

Man is lost. He doesn't know where he is. He doesn't know the way home. He isn't even sure there *is* a home to go to. He knows the right and can't do it. He does the wrong, and when his conscience tells him so, he starts arguing with his conscience and gets more muddled than ever. He wants peace in the world, but he drifts daily nearer to war. He wants the cure for cancer, but he spends most of his wealth making bigger and "better" bombs. He is lost. Sensible men admit it; and though there are others who say, "We are *not* lost," they are unconvincing. They are no more able to show the way to peace within, and peace in the world, than their neighbors who frankly admit our lost condition.

Christ is the Saviour. His main purpose in coming to this earth was to save men. He can deal with the guilt all decent men feel when they honestly look at their own past—the dirt in their thoughts and imaginations, if not in their deeds. He can enable us to do the right, swiftly and firmly, in every day as it comes and goes. He could save the world in its suicidal drift to mass destruction, and prove to us all that earth could "be fair and all men glad and wise."

Is he not well called "the Saviour"? If *he* can't save, who can?

35

How Does Christ Save?

HE BEGINS BY CONVINCING THE PEOPLE WHO THINK THEY DON'T need to be saved that they do. Millions of men deny their need of a Saviour. "What's wrong with me?" they say. "I don't do anybody any harm. I'm always doing good turns." So they say, and so they sincerely believe.

When these men meet Christ—that is, when they get a clear picture of him as given in the Bible and feel themselves in his presence—they know themselves unclean. Nobody need tell them so. They know it themselves, and they know at once that they need saving.

Nobody has the power to do this like Christ. Men are seldom convinced by argument that they are sinners. Most argument on this point is a waste of breath. Just get them to see what Christ is like and introduce them to him. They feel dirty at once. And because nobody wants to be saved until he knows he is lost, that is the first thing which must happen.

Then Christ goes to work. To a man who knows he is unclean and wants help, Christ says, "I can change your nature, if you will let me." If a man will take Christ into his life, his soiled past can be forgiven, and he will be given sound judgment and moral power in every day as it comes. He will cease to be the man he was and become another—the same personality but transformed. He is changed as a son, brother, husband, father, friend, workman, citizen—all relationships are affected by that change.

Consequently, his personal change affects society too. His home is different, his club, workshop—even his town and country to some extent, and (as the number of those changed multiply) this influence begins to affect the world.

Christ's power to save is unlimited. He hacks down the barrier of class, race, and color, and he leads also in the war against war. If people who call themselves Christians *really* followed him, his power would be more obvious than it is.

36

Do Decent People Need Saving?

THE WORD "DECENT" IS VAGUE. SOME PEOPLE USE IT OF ANYONE who keeps out of the hands of the police. But let us use it now in the best sense that we can. Let us think (as we did before) of people who are kind, neighborly, good citizens—but who have no use for religion.

All human nature is self-centered—even the nature of "nice" and "decent" people. Education makes no difference to this self-centeredness—except to put a veneer over it and make it less obvious. An observant man can see this self-centeredness every day—in himself, as well as in other people.

Here is a nice grandmother with snapshots of her grandchildren. She can bore you for an hour with them—and be weary in five minutes if you take out your own snapshots! How is your boy?" a nice and cultured gentleman said to me one day. "Let me tell you about mine." And he did, for thirty-five minutes!

The thing that is deeply wrong with human nature is not that some people commit adultery, and some steal, but that *all* of us are self-centered—the decent and the indecent, the nice and the nasty. Manners, polish, refinement, and culture only cover that disease, like rouge on the face of a woman dying of anemia. They can't affect the deadly disease underneath.

To be saved is to be saved from that disease. We all have it; therefore we all need to be saved. Some who claim to be saved have still got it and unconsciously bring religion into contempt. To see a man who claims to have been saved by Christ still wrapped up in himself, mean, unkind, faultfinding, gossipy— is to see a plain contradiction. When Christ saves us, self is no longer at the center; *he* is at the center. And when he is at the center, life is transformed.

Of course decent people need saving.

37

Why Do Christians Make So Much of the Cross?

CHRISTIANS NEVER SEEM ABLE TO PLUMB THE DEPTH OF MEANING in the Cross. It is no wonder that it has become the most sacred symbol of the faith in every branch of the Church. That God should suffer men to nail him on two pieces of wood staggers the minds of Christ's followers whenever they strip away their familiarity with it and look at it afresh. But here are a few of the things which make it unspeakably dear to them.

It shows how bad men are. Men don't like to admit their badness. Most of them think they are quite nice fellows and in no need of a Saviour. But Christ, the noblest soul who ever walked this earth, was crucified by men—not peculiarly *bad* men, not "the criminal types"; he was done to death by some of the "best" people of his day. Nothing like the Cross reveals the basic evil in men, and shows the vile depths to which our nature can sink. We are all guilty of the same sins which nailed Christ to the cross.

It shows how loving God is. Christ came to save. He meant to fight wickedness with love, and beat it. By mere power he could have blasted his enemies, but he let them murder him, and prayed for them as they did it. "I will conquer by this Cross," he said.

The Cross shows the supreme power of God to transform evil into good. In some senses, the Cross was the worst thing our race ever did. But God made it, at the same time, the best disclosure of his love to men. Dying to win our soiled and savage hearts, he showed us in one sublime deed what his heart is like through all eternity. We who are bewildered by earthquakes and disease germs, how can we help but wonder at times what God is like? If we really want to know, we must go to the Cross. The answer is clearest there. He loves like that.

The Cross shows to all Christians with insight how they must live. Self-assertion must be canceled out. Those who really follow Christ must be ready for the crucifixion of their proud demanding selves.

And all this is but the fringe of it. However much Christians make of the Cross, they never make enough of it.

What Do Christians Believe?

THE BEST BRIEF SUMMARY OF CHRISTIAN BELIEF IS IN THE HIS-
toric version of the Apostles' Creed. The Apostles didn't
make it, but it expresses in limited words what they themselves
believed and taught.

I believe in God the Father Almighty, Maker of heaven and
earth:

And in Jesus Christ His only Son our Lord, Who was conceived
by the Holy Ghost, Born of the Virgin Mary, Suffered under Pontius
Pilate, Was crucified, dead, and buried, He descended into hell;
The third day He rose again from the dead, He ascended into
heaven, And sitteth on the right hand of God the Father Almighty;
From thence He shall come to judge the quick and the dead.

I believe in the Holy Ghost; The holy Catholic Church; The
Communion of Saints; the Forgiveness of sins; The Resurrection
of the body, And the Life everlasting.

Three phrases in the creed have been debated more of recent
years than any others: "Born of the Virgin Mary," "He descended into hell," and "the resurrection of the body." We
ought to look at each of them in turn.

39

Must I Believe in the Virgin Birth?

There are some Christians—they are very few in the millions
of believers—who find it hard to believe that Christ was born of
a virgin. They know that this teaching is in the Bible and the

early creeds, but it borders on the impossible for them. They can't see the *necessity* for it. Nobody else, they say, was born of a virgin. Why should Christ be? He is more our example if he wasn't so born.

We need to see this event in the setting of his life as a whole. Christians who deny the Virgin Birth believe that Christ was the Son of God, lived a sinless life, rose from the dead. . . . If they believe all this, it is hard to understand why the Virgin Birth should seem impossible to them. If they are convinced that he was a person apart, lived differently from all others, and made an impact on history unparalleled in our race, why should it be incredible to them that his entrance into human life should be as unusual as his leaving it?

No doubt—if God had so chosen—Christ could have been who he was, and the Saviour of the race, even if he had had a human father. No doubt, also, a man seeking his way to conviction in the Christian religion would do well (if he finds the Virgin Birth difficult to believe) to defer judgment on it until he is better acquainted with Christ in his own experience and comes to know (as he surely will) that no human category is large enough for this unique person. Then this part of the ancient creed will take its fitting place in his mind, and he will better judge whether the normal tests of science are rightly applied to the life and work of Jesus Christ.

And, as he broods on the mystery of it, his love of science will remind him that nature (in the widest sense) has many ways of begetting new life besides that of normal human generation, and he may wonder why he can't believe the agelong conviction of the Church that the Holy Ghost conceived within the virgin's womb and brought the Christ to birth in that way.

Why Should Christ Descend into Hell?

THE WORD "HELL" IS USED, EVEN IN CHRISTIAN LITERATURE, WITH a double meaning. Normally, it is employed for the place (or state) of firm separation from God—the opposite of heaven. But sometimes it is used as the equivalent of "hades"—the place of all departed spirits, not yet set in their eternal abode.

Precisely what the early fathers who shaped the Apostles' Creed believed about this phrase is still a subject of discussion among scholars, and even the present interpretation of it differs in various branches of the Church. Some think that Christ challenged Satan and all his powers in the central "citadel" of hell. Some think that his mission there was particularly to those who had followed the best light they had in their generation, but who, having lived before his earthly ministry, had had no opportunity to respond to the best of all.

It is this second interpretation which fosters the hope in some Christians that Christ still has a ministry on the other side of death. Millions die never having heard of him. Millions more have heard of him, but he is little more than a name to them; they have never felt the conscious impact of his love, nor traced some of the loveliest things in the world to his influence. Even in countries classified as "Christian," thousands of children grow up in homes from which Christ is virtually excluded, and hear his name only in blasphemy.

It is unthinkable that the God whom Christ came to reveal could allow these multitudes to miss their highest bliss because of the accident or misfortune of their birth. A God of love is compelled by his nature to pursue with the offer of salvation all creatures made in his own image. Why Christ descended into hell—and precisely what "hell" used in this context means—

is a mystery not likely to be cleared up on this earth, but the constantly repeated phrase has this overtone in the minds of many of the faithful, and leads them to the conviction that death does not end the ministries of grace.

41

What Do You Mean by "The Resurrection of the Body"?

WE MEAN THE SURVIVAL OF PERSONALITY. CHRISTIANS DO NOT BE-lieve that individuality ends at death (as some Eastern religions do) and that man is "lost" in Nirvana, or outer space, or "in the ocean of being." You are you and I am I, and death will not alter that.

"But why the resurrection of the *body?*" people persist. "We can believe that the personality survives death without believ-ing that the body does."

Of course—if you think of the dead body as it is put into the earth. The immediate successors of the Apostles, who first formulated the Creed, were not so foolish as to suppose that the bodies of Christians remained undecayed until a general resur-rection, and were then claimed again by their spirits, which had been temporarily dispossessed.

We have no knowledge of personality apart from *form*. It is, indeed, almost inconceivable to us. Try to think of anyone with-out a form—even God. You can't. You may think of him as light, or as some upright blur, but the mind fails before it. Always, we must think of personality in a *form*.

Christians believe that personalities survive in a form, a form in some way recognizable as theirs, and related, therefore, to the body that was part of them on this earth. They do not think that the material particles of the discarded body compose again, but that the surviving form will be a transformation of the earthly body and identifiable as such. As we need a body in this life to express our personality, so we shall need a "form" for the same purpose in the next.

The resurrection body of Christ is a guide to faith. It was independent of doors and distances. It could be mistaken at a hurried glance, but was recognized and known by all who loved him.

This is most helpful, for the belief that we shall know and recognize those we have loved when we meet them on the other side of death is a precious part of the Christian faith.

42

Is Christ Our Pattern?

SO CHRISTIANS FIRMLY BELIEVE. IT FOLLOWS, INEVITABLY, FROM their conviction as to who he was. If Christ was God visiting this planet in person, his life, his teaching, his influence, his death, all become the standard for those who would follow him.

We have already recognized why his coming in person was required by the love he had for us. Nature of itself cannot adequately reveal God. Nature speaks with two voices; the boa constrictor is part of nature as well as the lamb. If we consider only the *lovely* things in nature—sunsets, flowers, stars, and trees—they are still not high or "plastic" enough to reveal God. However much greater God must be than human beings, nothing *less* than a person could disclose him to persons, and therefore he took upon himself "the form of a servant," and came as a man.

He is always ahead of us. Only slowly (even in the Church) do we realize his demands and recognize how we fail by his tests. For centuries (even in civilized lands) women were held to be inferior to men, though Christ treated them always with special respect, and it is laid down in the Bible that "in him" there is neither male nor female. Still more slowly do we come to see that he is against barriers of race and class and color, and that war is a contradiction of his will. The clear test of progress is our approximation to his way of life.

But we must consider now the dependability of the Bible, because it is in the Bible that we study the record of Christ's earthly life. We do not learn of him *only* in the Bible; as we live with him in our minds and hearts, we gather the most personal and precious knowledge by our own experience. Yet even this is based, in the first place, on what we learned of him in the Holy Book.

How should we read the Bible? Can we depend upon it as a revelation of God?

43

Can We Believe the Bible?

MOST CERTAINLY—IF WE ARE CAREFUL OF THE SENSE IN WHICH we use the word "believe."

There are sixty-six "books" or "writings" bound up in the Bible. It is, indeed, a little library all in itself. Its composition covered hundreds of years and it was originally written in Hebrew and Greek.

Most forms of literature are included in the Bible: history, allegory, poetry, prophecy, letters, laws, proverbs, and parables.

Now, if we use the word "believe" to mean a factual or scientific accuracy in every phrase, we shall go astray. How could you read any poetry that way? Most history, too, is written from "a point of view." And the details of parables are usually deliberately made up, for the truth does not lie on the surface; people listen because all people like a story, and it is only afterwards that the truth is seen, not in the incidents of the narrative, but in the deeper meaning.

Most people know the parable of the prodigal son. Almost certainly, Jesus made the story up. He couldn't have given the address of the father in his story, because the human father lived only in his imagination. But who cares about that? The deep divine truth of the parable, the precious unalterable fact that should mean everything to all the teeming millions of men and women in the world, is that *God is like that father*. He is loving, wise in his dealings with his children, giving them freedom but requiring obedience to his moral commands, uncompromising with wrongdoing but ready to meet sincere repentance with pardon.

Now that is the kind of truth to seek in the Bible. We shall not find it if we get bogged down in endless arguments about whether a man can live in the belly of a whale, or whether the sun ever "stood still," but only if we ask what this book is telling us about God.

And what this book—understood as a growing revelation—tells us about God we can most surely believe.

44

What Is Meant by a "Growing Revelation?"

JESUS KNEW MORE ABOUT GOD THAN MOSES—EVEN THOUGH MOSES knew more about God than any other man living in his time. Nor should that surprise us. If—as Christians believe—Christ was God on earth, it does not belittle Moses to say that Jesus knew more than Moses did about his heavenly Father.

All through human history God has been seeking to show himself to men and women. Some races have been more sensitive to his revelations than others—the Hebrews especially—and (even among them) some men were more sensitive than the rest. We generally call these men "prophets," though the chief thing about them was not any power they had to foretell future events, but their power to see more of the nature of God.

The degree to which God can show his nature to a man depends on that man's spiritual sensitivity and obedience, and when we talk of a "growing revelation" we mean that men saw more and more as the centuries passed by. They saw, for instance, that he didn't care only for *their* tribes, but cared for *all* men. They saw that his concern for holiness wasn't satisfied by religious ceremonies but by purity of heart and mind. The teaching of the prophets did not die with them, but became part of the spiritual treasure of the race, and when Jesus came, he confirmed their great insights (or God's revelations to them) and added more.

That is why one of the later books in the Bible opens with the word, "God, who gave to our forefathers many varied glimpses of the truth in the words of the prophets, has now . . . given us the Truth in His Son." (Heb. 1:1.)

Consequently, we find the truth of God all through the Bible, but supremely in the life and teaching of Jesus; and when we are in any doubt about the divine will, we bring it to an ultimate test in the revelation of Christ. If, for instance, in the lovely psalms we come upon something quite unlovely, and find expressed a bitter and revengeful spirit, we do not feel superior to the author (for we have felt the same emotions ourselves), but we say, "This was not a true interpretation of God's character, for Jesus taught us to forgive the people who do us wrong!"

45

How Should We Read the Bible?

OUR READING OF ANY BOOK IS AFFECTED BY THE STATE OF MIND in which we undertake it. If a man comes to the Bible believing that the Old Testament is largely unimportant Jewish History and Jewish Law, and the New Testament a story (largely legendary) about Jesus Christ and the early Church, he will not profit much by his reading. His mind is barricaded against the deeper wisdom the Bible has to give.

But if he comes to it impressed by the fact that it has fed the souls of millions of people of all types through many hundreds of years, he will treat it reverently, and with a sense of honest quest. If, moreover, he has the humble desire in his heart for any supernatural aid which may be available in his study, it will soon begin to show him hidden treasure, and his longing to understand it better will increase.

The Bible is not an easy book for beginners. It is best read under the direction of one who knows the inwardness of it, or by the aid of those groups and organizations which publish notes on selected passages. There are parts of it which are very dull to all but experts. Yet there is no book which more repays the right kind of persistence, and in the end, to those who read it as it is meant to be read, it becomes the Book of all books and life's greatest treasure.

That should not surprise us. The book which tells of God's dealings with the most spiritually sensitive people of ancient times, the book which alone contains the record of his Son's life on earth, the book which records the founding of the Christian Church must ever be a book apart. To get beneath the sometimes difficult surface of it, to mine deep into its unearthly wisdom, to store one's memory with quarried fragments of it, is to spend time at its maximum use.

Hurriedly to leaf the Book over at random is to court confusion. To penetrate to its heart is to understand why people call it "the Word of God."

46

Can We Be Sure of Christ's Words?

CHRIST SPOKE IN ARAMAIC AND WHAT HE SAID WAS WRITTEN DOWN in Greek; moreover, nearly forty years may have gone by before it was written down. That, however, was less serious for accuracy in the East than it would have been in the West, for learning by memory was common then and there, and an oral record was much more dependable among those devout Jews than it would be among us. People who saw and heard Christ stand right behind our record.

Moreover, Christ spoke in the thought-forms and images of the period. Naturally. How else would the people understand? All speech, to be understood, must be in the thought-form of its period. Imagine the people of two thousand years ago faced with metaphors drawn from radio and sputniks!

Not many people in the world—proportionately speaking—read the New Testament in the original Greek. They read it in their own language, and so they are reading a translation of a translation. When we raise the question, therefore, "Can we be sure of Christ's words?" we must see the question in its setting and focus it aright.

The one intelligent sense we can give to the question is this: "Do we understand Christ's meaning?" To that an emphatic "Yes" can be given. The teaching in all four gospels holds together. Clearly, too, we are dealing with the same personality in each. Much will be missed by a hurried reader, and many deep shades of meaning yield themselves only to the most prayerful study. But—as we concluded before—we are left in no doubt on all the things we need to know for life. God is at work. God is holy. God is love. His best human name is Father. He has a sublime purpose for the world and everyone in it. We are morally responsible beings and some day we must give account. God is merciful to those who are sincerely sorry for the evil they have done, but he forces no one to repentance.

No humble Christian claims to understand the inwardness of all Christ's words, but he claims to know all he needs for the voyage of life.

70

What About the Parts of the Bible
We Don't Understand?

THERE ARE PARTS OF THE BIBLE NO ONE FULLY UNDERSTANDS. There are other parts we understand without seeing very clearly why they are in the Bible—for instance, the long family trees, details of Jewish ceremonial laws, records of what appear to be unimportant tribal wars, and dark prophetic sayings whose historical setting is lost in the mists of time.

It is well to remember that these things had a value centuries ago, even if they are obscure to us now, and even now an inner meaning sometimes breaks from these passages which can strangely help us in our own needs and in our own times. But it is best to know the Bible so intimately that we can turn in it freely to whatever we need—not seeking comfort only but seeking the whole counsel of God. Here is wisdom. Here is the timeless message of the Living God making itself relevant to each generation as it comes and goes. The Bible is never outdated. It is always the world's "best seller."

Perhaps the simplest illustration of how to deal with the parts of the Bible you still can't understand after study (and after seeking help from those who know it better than you do) is this. Treat the Bible like your dinner. If you have a chop for dinner, you leave the bone on the plate. There is value, of course, in bones, but you can't get it out with your knife and fork. Yet the rest of the chop makes a wonderful meal. You have your fill and it is all good food.

The Bible is there to feed your soul. It is able to do so—beyond all question and beyond all measure. God speaks in a unique way through this book. Without its revelation, this world would be dark beyond description. So know it, and use it, and it will be what it claims to be—"a lamp to your feet."

But now we must turn to another way of knowing God. We must consider prayer.

PRAYER

48

Is It My Duty to Pray?

IT IS MUCH MORE YOUR PRIVILEGE THAN YOUR DUTY. IF YOU WERE ever summoned to the White House to meet the President, you could speak, if you wished, of the duty to obey, but you would much more naturally speak of the privilege of being asked: It is your *privilege* to pray. It is the greatest privilege any human being enjoys.

Moreover, it is one of the chief ways by which you can know God. When we spoke about the venture or "gamble" with which personal religion begins, we said that it involved prayer, and when a man who has never prayed (or not since childhood) begins to pray, he can feel foolish. It may seem like talking into space. Some men would rather be caught stealing than caught praying.

Yet if a man persists, he will cease to feel foolish. He will begin to feel that it "does him good." The question may cross his mind as to whether prayer is some form of autosuggestion (and we must look closely at that in a moment), but he is almost certain to feel that it "does him good." His days go better after a bit of honest prayer. He is less in danger of "going off the deep end," both at home and at work. He is easier to live with, happier—in some ways healthier.

As time passes, he grows more sure that his prayers are heard and answered. Things happen which he would have called "coincidence" at one time, but he can't call them that any more. He senses a pattern in them and a purpose behind them. The

73

conviction grows in him that, although he is so small and God
is so great, the millions of people who have believed in prayer
through the ages are right. God can be reached this way and has
a personal concern about men and women.

It is almost too staggering to believe, but the man who persists in prayer comes to believe it. He sees that to talk of prayer
as "duty" is half-silly. It is pure privilege—the very highest
privilege of all.

49

Is Prayer Autosuggestion?

PEOPLE WHO BELIEVE THAT PRAYER IS JUST AUTOSUGGESTION ARE
quite ready to concede that a man who prays thinks that it does
him "good." "It *does* do him good," they assert, "though not
quite for the reasons he supposes. It isn't God working on him.
It does anybody good to think hopeful, happy, and grateful
thoughts, and when a man fills his mind with these (as so many
do in prayer) the thoughts themselves react on the mind which
entertains them and he feels 'good.' But it is his own thought
which is doing it, not God."

The fact that it does us good to think hopeful, happy thoughts
doesn't disprove God. Christian prayer at its highest is not
asking for things, but concentrating on God. The result of
God's entrance into any man's life is set down in the Bible as
love, joy, peace, patience, kindness, goodness, integrity, humility, and self-control (Gal. 5:22-3). When God comes into a
man's life, these come with him. No man keeps on praying who
comes to think prayer is just autosuggestion, and most people
who keep thinking "high" thoughts just because they wish them
to be true usually get weary of deceiving themselves.

In Christian prayer it isn't merely the thought which does us good, but the thought which becomes the channel of divine power. Moreover, what of those external happenings we mentioned—too frequent to be coincidences—which people recognize so often as answers to prayer? Those are not the fruit of our own thinking.

A man was once shown a few flint axheads by a friend interested in archaeology and told that they were man-made. He couldn't believe it. He felt that his friend's imagination had run away with him. But he went to a museum and saw hundreds and hundreds of them, with the same features repeated again and again. He knew then that the idea of their being man-made wasn't imagination and their likeness wasn't coincidence. A designing mind was behind them.

So it is with our answers to prayer. A few could be pushed away as coincidences, but not these multitudes. There is a designing mind behind them. Prayer is not just autosuggestion.

50

Can Prayer Change Things?

MANY PEOPLE BELIEVE THAT, WHATEVER VALUE PRAYER MAY have to lift a man's feelings, it cannot possibly affect physical events, because the universe runs by unalterable law. If the universe did not run by unalterable law life would be impossible. If fire burned today but didn't burn tomorrow, if water boiled at one temperature today and froze at the same temperature tomorrow, neither man nor beast could survive. Life is possible only because of these unchanging laws, and we should be grateful for their unchanging character—even if they seem to cancel out some of our prayers.

But—before we conclude they do that—let us remember again what we noticed when we were considering the miracles of Christ. Laws interact with other laws. Iron will neither float nor hang in the air, but we have liners like floating palaces crossing the wide oceans and mighty planes flying over all the continents of the world. Planes don't break the law of gravity, for there are laws of aerodynamics as well.

There are spiritual laws, too, which are not as firmly separated from physical laws as we thought at one time. It is likely (as we saw) that some of Christ's miracles were performed by his use of higher laws. Scientists are themselves abandoning the old ideas of "cause and effect," if by those words are meant some completely rigid sequences which nothing can alter. One of them has said "the old foundations of physics have broken up," and that they can no longer talk of mechanical explanations, if only because they do not now know what they mean by "mechanics."

Perhaps we are helped a little here by what is called "psychosomatic" sickness. People are sometimes made ill, not by a germ, but by a thought, a fear—and a thought or fear far deeper than the conscious mind. The effect is physical—sometimes awful and ugly—but the cause is mental and spiritual.

People are sometimes cured that way too. There are many senses in which prayer changes things.

51

Is "Thy Will Be Done" the Only Proper Prayer?

SOME PEOPLE THINK IT IS. AMONG THOSE WHO THINK THIS WAY, there are those whose spiritual life is shallow and who almost want a reason for not praying at all (I'm leaving everything to God), and some whose spiritual life is very deep but whose prayer is so completely adoration that it seems to have no place for petition at all.

Prayer—as we have seen—is fellowship with God. *It is being with him.* He made us for friendship, and his fatherly heart is always seeking our close companionship.

The sublime fruit of this friendship for men and women is that they grow like him. All people grow to some extent like those they love, admire, and live with, and one of the most wonderful things about human beings is that they can grow like God. If, therefore, people neglect prayer on the apparently pious ground that they can always trust God "to do the right thing," they are missing, nonetheless, the fruit of his companionship and are not growing like the Lord they profess to love.

We can take (without irreverence) a comparison from human family life. Christ encouraged us to do so, and more than once taught things about God by pictures drawn from a human home. Would any normal father be glad if his son never wanted his company, never asked him for anything (even though he knew already what the boy hoped for), never sought his opinion, or judgment, or guidance, or encouragement? It would be an appalling experience to any normal father. Nothing could compensate him for the loss. "How can I overcome the boy's estrangement from me?" would be his constant wonder.

And that is a picture of the aching heart of God. His effort to overcome the estrangement led Christ to earth and to the cross.

52

Can Prayer Alter God's Mind?

IT IS GOD'S MIND ALWAYS TO BLESS US, THOUGH OUR SIN AND indifference often prevent the blessing coming through. But perhaps the following true story will make clear in its simple way how a blessing God cannot give us this week he may give us next.

Years ago a Manchester businessman had a son named Ted. He had always intended to send Ted to Cambridge. Indeed, the boy was entered at one of the colleges and was looking forward to going with eagerness.

But in his late teens Ted seemed to go wild. He made the wrong friends. He ignored his studies. He was rude to his mother, and occasionally came home tipsy. One night, in the privacy of their own room, Ted's father said to his wife, "I'm not sending Ted to Cambridge. If he acts like this under our own roof, what will he be like at the university? He must come into the business, and work all the while under my eye."

Ted was mad when he was told and sullen for a week. But then something remarkable happened to him. He went to a youth group where they discussed religion in a rational way, and he got deeply interested. Indeed, he went further. When he was told that interest was not enough and that if a man would *know* these things he must "commit himself" and practice religion, he took the plunge and was a different person within a month.

He told his parents about it. "I know I coming straight into the business, Dad," he said, "but I'm going to make you proud of me." A week later Ted's father said quietly to his wife, "I'm going to send Ted to Cambridge. The boy's all right. He'll make the most of the opportunity."

God's will to bless us is constant, but whether he can or not often depends on us.

53

Why Do We Have to Persist in Prayer?

IT PERPLEXES SOME PEOPLE WHY THE BIBLE TEACHES US TO PERSIST in prayer. They think a loving and all-wise Father would know what we need without being asked and (even if he liked to be asked) wouldn't need to be asked again. Why must we go on asking for the same thing? Doesn't he *want* to give?

Sometimes we ask for things which God knows would not be for our good. Sometimes we ask for things we ought not be praying for at all. Prayer is not a substitute for work. A student who neglects his studies and then prays to God that he may pass his examination is trying to make the Almighty the accomplice of his own laziness.

Sometimes, when we ask for something we know God wants to give and yet it doesn't come, the delay is caused by somebody else's free will. Imagine a mother praying for her bad son to be changed. *She* wants it. *God* wants it. But perhaps the years go by and he isn't changed. God never *forces* goodness on anyone. A will firmly set to evil can withstand even God. But the mother should still persist. The combined constraint of a good mother and the great God are enormous, and all the time the bad man will feel upon him the pull of better things.

Sometimes God keeps us waiting in order to increase our appreciation when the answer to our prayer finally comes. If he gave us any good thing we asked for on our first light asking, we would not value the answer as we ought. Suppose a child in the family asked to play with your gold watch or a Ming vase.

79

Would you let him—even if he cried for it? "He must wait," you would say, "till he can appreciate its worth." It is like that with our prayers sometimes. Half-convinced that there may be something in religion, men have prayed to God to "reveal" himself to them, but when they see no vision, hear no voice, feel no immediate and mighty change, they give it up. "There's nothing in it," they say. Their swift abandonment of the quest proves that their desire was not deep. They admit that to master a symphony might take months of study, but they expect to "pick up" God in a few minutes.

One way of proving our seriousness is our persistence in prayer. Those who persist come to know God, even if they do not always know on this earth the divine purpose which said a loving "No" to their prayer.

54

Is It True That Prayer Heals?

IT WOULD BE MORE PRECISE TO SAY THAT PRAYER CAN BE A channel of God's power in healing. All healing comes from God. Most of it, in the modern world, comes through doctors, though God sometimes heals people by other means when doctors abandon hope for them. Not all the doctors admit in such cases that God has done it. If they are unbelievers, or if (though believers) they think that God won't work without them, they comment on the astonishing happening by saying, "Well, these things *do* occur sometimes. It's just one of those things."

But if we leave this aspect of the matter aside (if only because it is still in sharp dispute), there are other aspects of prayer and healing on which almost all thoughtful people agree. Mind and spirit and body are knit together. No sensible person doubts now that a state of mind can cause sickness, or predispose us towards it, or hinder the good work the doctor is doing when he is trying to make us well.

A life opened to God in faithful prayer is opened to agencies of healing beyond the range of medicine and surgery. A man who prays properly must pray without hate in his heart to anyone. (That gets rid of resentments—a mass of them in some minds.) A man who prays properly must ask forgiveness for his sins, and God has promised to forgive us our sins when we are sincerely penitent. (That gets rid of the deep sense of guilt in many minds—even if it is in so low a level of the mind that a man is barely aware of it.) Hope, trust, confidence, courage, all enter a mind into which God comes; and fear, guilt, and worry can be banished. All that this could mean for healing is beyond our power to compute, but it would be immense.

Without doubt, the right kind of prayer is related to healing.

55

Does God Speak to Us When We Pray?

YES. THAT IS WHY THE MORE IMPORTANT PART OF PRAYER IS THE listening part of it—not what *we* say to God but what God says to us.

If a man will try this, if he makes his mind quiet and thinks on the great holy God and then listens, he will be surprised how many voices are speaking inside him. Indeed, it may seem like pandemonium at times. Memory, wishes, fears—they all find a voice in turn, and sometimes they all talk together. Nothing clearly to be recognized as the voice of God will sound inside him, and his impulse will be to give it up.

But if that man persists, if he meditates on the Bible and on the kind of God whom Christ revealed and never minds the time it takes, another voice will awake inside him, a voice as quiet as some of the others were noisy, and one which carries a strange assurance with it. It speaks with authority and *you are sure that it isn't you.*

People who have given much of their life to listening to God (like the old prophets and the saints) hear this voice most clearly and their writings and insights have become part of the treasure of our race. But ordinary people can listen to God too. Perhaps nothing will come to them of benefit for the whole race, but much will come of benefit to their own life and home and job. A man will hear himself condemned for the shabby things he has done, or is doing, or wants to do. He will find himself encouraged in other things, and strengthened to go on with them though nobody else notices, or notices only to criticize. Sometimes he will be told quite plainly to do certain things—to help particular people or to watch certain situations. When he obeys this guidance, things will often fit together so strangely that he won't doubt that somebody else is working with him, and when this becomes part of a man's life and happens often, he builds up an enormous amount of experience and develops a conviction that nothing can overthrow.

A man needs this kind of experience and total conviction to face the problems we have to face next, because we have come now to the darkest part of the road.

56

Could a God of Love Have Made a World Like This?

THE WORLD IN WHICH WE LIVE IS FULL OF CONTRADICTIONS. WE have mentioned already many of the lovely things it contains, but there are many others which are far from lovely.

Think of the wickedness in men which has expressed itself in wars, persecutions, slavery, torturings, concentration camps, and gas chambers. Civilization often seems only a thin veneer covering something worse in men than the nature of a wild beast.

Yet although these are the cause of our greatest pain and horror, they are not the cause of our greatest perplexity, because they are all traceable to the evil in man. There are other evils which seem built into the very structure of creation, and almost to leap out of the hand of God. Think of one species of animal or fish feeding on another. Think of the diphtheria germ and other germs of vile disease, which all seem to be part of creation too. Think of earthquakes, epidemics, famines, and floods.

Everything which lives is subject to disease. Men and women, birds and beasts, fish and flowers, trees and shrubs—nothing is exempt. Life seems poisoned near the fount. To look at life honestly, and in its wholeness, is a solemn undertaking for anybody. It isn't *obviously* the work of a God of love.

Nor is there an easy answer to any of these questions. Nowhere is the Christian more frankly agnostic than when he faces these problems. Light falls on some of them. To others he must frankly say, "I do not know."

But the people with alternative explanations are in a worse

plight. Those who say that there is no purpose in the world and it all "just happened" strain our credulity to breaking point. Could this amazing and intricate world have just happened? They admit "purpose" in all the *parts* of nature—in bees and beasts and men, for instance—and none in the *whole!* The people who say that a devil made the universe have a harder task to explain the good in the world than we have to explain the evil. What a devil, to have made the lovely things which we enjoy!

If—for other impressive reasons—we believe that there is a good God behind the universe, let us approach the problem honestly and humbly, and see how a God of love could have made a world like this.

57

What Was God's Purpose in It All?

GOD MADE MEN AND WOMEN FOR FELLOWSHIP WITH HIMSELF. He made us (the Bible says) "in his own image," and however vastly greater God must be than anyone whom he has made, we can at least catch a glimpse, in the thought, feeling, and will which blend in our own nature, of the mighty being who is behind all things.

In making us for virtue and for loving fellowship with himself, God made us free. He *had* to. Only the free can be good, and love is only acceptable when it is freely given. It is of course a *limited* freedom; we cannot pluck the sun from the sky, or change the order of the seasons, or do many other things. But within its limited orbit, our freedom is real. We can withhold our love. We can do evil and not good. We can hate and lie and torture; something inside tells us that all three are wrong, but we are free to do them. For the purpose God had in mind, he had to make us free.

Robots cannot love. Puppets are not persons. The great God could have filled his world with machine-like creatures who would always have reacted in precise ways to precise conditions, but they could not love and they could not be good. Hence he took the risk of evil, and the evil came. It has grown. Some believe that it has tainted our nature. To call this evil (as men do) just the "survival of the beast" in us is too shallow and is unjust to the beasts. No animal is guilty of the evil of men. When we think of the wickedness of war, persecution, torture (and all the other vile things we listed as the action of free men), we speak to our own shame.

Men argue sometimes that we are not free, that whatever we do is the result of "pressures" upon us; but no one has ever been able to prove this point. Certainly the awareness of all sane men is against them. We *feel* free. It is true that we feel the "pressures" also, but at the last we *choose*. "I couldn't help it!" is a weakling's cry. Nor do the the people who say that we are not free act on their own conviction. If their house is broken into, they prosecute the burglar as soon as anyone else; it doesn't occur to them to let him off because he couldn't help it.

58

What About the Pain in the World?

IT IS THE AWFUL AMOUNT OF PAIN IN THE WORLD WHICH PRE-vents some people from believing in a God of love. No wonder! When we put together the agony of man and beast spread across the wide world, the mind shudders and quails before it all.

But don't let us make a grim problem grimmer than it is.

Fortunately, we can't put pains "together." Nobody really suffers someone else's pain. Pains can't be added up. The greatest pain endured in the world was endured by the *one* person who suffered most. Some people believe—if you put together spiritual, mental, and physical pain as well—that that one person was Jesus Christ. But that is personal opinion. We cannot *know*.

The pain of animals, it seems, is exaggerated by animal lovers. Folk fond of animals (as I am) transfer to animals the agony a human being would suffer in similar circumstances, but fortunately the nervous systems of animals are different from ours and they know little of the anticipations which afflict the members of our race. Most animals enjoy living, and swift death from another animal seeking food need not be drawn-out agony.

Moreover, all thoughtful people realize that pain is a friend as well as a foe. If that diseased appendix in my body had given no pain it would have burst before I knew I was ill. Pain warned me; it rang the bell and saved my life. Pain is a monitor of health. A coal miner was awarded substantial compensation a while ago because an accident in the pit had strangely robbed him of the power to feel pain. He could put his hand on a hot stove and it wouldn't hurt. He couldn't *feel* things when he picked them up. They rightly paid him for his lack of pain.

None of this dismisses the problem of unfruitful pain, but it is helping us to get the difficulties focused. Searing and prolonged pain is awful; no metaphor or illustration can alter that. But it opens the way into the subject to remember that pain *is* sometimes our friend.

59

Can Pain Ever Be Justified?

"JUSTIFIED" IS AN AWKWARD WORD IN THIS CONNECTION. ADMIT-ting the deep mystery of pain, and with no foolish expectation of "explaining it away," we have already seen that pain has a most valued usefulness when it serves as the guardian of our health. Without any sentimental romancing, we can see other things too. Pain draws out enormous kindness and pity in this hard world.

I am writing this as a patient in a hospital. People all around me twist and turn in pain. I have my own heavy disabilities to bear. They have just taken a dead body past the foot of my bed. Yet the love and care of the doctors and chaplain and nurses, the medical technicians, the ward orderlies, domestics and por-ters, are so wonderful that it is almost worth being ill to see such love in human nature. It is hard to say it (and some will resent it), but it would not be a better world if it were made up entirely of people who had everything they wanted, and were robbed of this deep compassion which flows around me now.

Many people of spiritual insight believe that suffering came into the world with sin, that when man exercised his freedom against the counsel of God, suffering and disease were two of the consequences. This would not mean, of course, that suffering is a punishment for *personal* sin. Too many innocent children suffer for us to believe that old lie. But it would mean that sin and suffering came into our *race,* and good and bad alike are exposed to the possibility of pain.

Nor can it be denied that some people are able to turn their suffering into triumph. I look around me and see two things happening in this ward. With the same pain, some men are becoming bitter and resentful and a problem to the rest, and others are so brave and trustful that I lie amazed at what God can do in a pain-wracked body. I see it again—in this life, what matters isn't so much what happens *to* us, as what happens *in* us. The same thing can happen *to* two different people and a precisely opposite thing can happen *in* them.

But couldn't an almighty God have made a better world than this?

60

Couldn't an Almighty God Do Better Than This?

WE MUSTN'T GET MUDDLED BY THE WORD "ALMIGHTY." BEING almighty doesn't mean that God can do everything, He can't contradict the sense of things and make a square circle, or a cubic ball, or an aged infant. When we complain at times about the world, we seem to want it both ways. We want water we can swim in but not drown in, fire which will warm the house but not burn the children when we leave it unguarded, air which will give us life but the absence of which will not cause our death. We should prefer pain also which would guard our health but never approach the unbearable.

But it is a stern world in which God has placed us, and we have made it sterner by our racial follies and wickedness. God works with us for the cure of incurable disease, but we pour out our wealth and brains on making bigger and "better" bombs. The same world-wide research and expenditure which has been lavished on war might have given us the cure of cancer long before this. Yet we can be grateful for the medical research which is being done and recognize that it is *pain* which puts the chief passion into all that work.

Perhaps nothing so much as pain reminds us so sharply that ours is a world astray. If we could be perfectly comfortable in a world so full of warring wickedness, it would be an even worse world than it is. If pain and sin are linked at some deep racial level, the pain will keep before us the sin we would so cheerfully ignore. That some people have more to bear than others is one of the darkest mysteries of all, though I have often been impressed by the contrast between the courage of those who are bearing the pain and the denunciations of God from those healthy people who are just looking on.

There is a deep word in the Bible which suggests that God can *use* suffering, that even Christ himself was made "perfect" through it (Heb. 5:8), though this was suffering he had willingly accepted and not disease. It outruns our understanding, but those who bear an unlifting burden can pray, at least, that God will fashion in them something worthy of the price which pain has paid.

61

Isn't God Against Disease?

GOD IS TOTALLY AGAINST DISEASE. IT MAKES NONSENSE OF MOST of Christ's life on earth to take any other view. Only those who have taken care to examine the gospels with this point in mind realize how much of Christ's ministry was taken up with healing.

Without overpressing the parallel, we may compare disease in the body with sin in the soul. No Christian doubts that God is completely opposed to the latter; not all realize with the same conviction his battle with disease.

People talk at times of sickness and disease as being "the will of God," but it does not prevent them waiting on the doctor for a cure. It is only "the will of God" in the sense that God created the world order in which sin and disease were possible. But man has misused his freedom. So sin has come into the world, and sickness and disease with it. But God is not more opposed to sin than he is opposed to sickness. His will for men and women is perfect health of body and of soul.

"Why then," people ask, "doesn't he banish sickness with one stroke of his almighty power?" If this question troubles you, ask yourself another one, "Why doesn't he banish sin in the same way?" The answer is, "Because our freedom is involved." The moment God forced us to goodness, we should be robots and not men.

At some level, our freedom is involved in sickness as well— not in precisely the same way, not in a fashion easily recognizable, but in the fact that we sometimes break God's laws of health through folly or ignorance and the penalties follow (even where we are in no way to blame, as with little children and many adults too). God is fighting disease as he is fighting sin. All who really heal are his colleagues. Medical research students receive his aid—whether they are aware of it or not. He does not write the answers on the heavens for us, because he treats us as persons and works with us in fellowship. But he is *against* disease.

Thus, while some of the explanations elude us, those who go to him in suffering know how real is his help.

62

What of Earthquakes, Famines, Floods, and Germs?

NATURAL DISASTERS ARE WORSE IN SOME WAYS THAN THOSE EVILS which can be traced to the wickedness of men. Although the amount of suffering they cause is quite small in comparison with the result of human sin (war, torturing, persecutions, etc.) they are harder to explain by anyone who believes in a God of love.

But do not let us make them harder than they are. Earthquakes, it seems, are due usually to a "fault" in the earth's crust. Most of the areas where these "faults" occur are known, but (sometimes by overcrowding and sometimes by folly) people build their homes again on the "fault." Volcanoes are vent-holes for the burning interior of our earth. Again, most of them are known, but people still insist on living in their dangerous locality. The lava is barely cool on Vesuvius before the people are moving back.

Famines are sometimes the fruit of a deliberate misuse of the good earth, which turns the sinned-against soil into a vast dustbowl. Floods are being turned to man's service. Caught in a reservoir, men are using the torrential waters in the steady irrigation of what would otherwise be a desert waste. Much that once seemed utterly evil in nature turns out to have an unexpected use, or to be the misdirection of something essentially good.

People bent upon proving that there is no good God behind the universe often point to disease germs as being sufficient proof in themselves that no loving heart called the world into being. But we do not know enough about the origin of disease germs to be completely emphatic on the point. Some research students are of the opinion that worry, hate, and fear can so alter the chemical constitution of certain fluids in the body that they change harmless bacteria into virulent bacteria. We base no argument on this opinion. We mention it only to remind ourselves (and others) that there are too many things we do not understand about the world to leave us certain that a good God can be dismissed from it.

63

What of the Suffering of Animals?

THERE ARE SENSES IN WHICH OUR DIFFICULTIES COME TO THEIR climax here. If suffering in men is in some way the fruit of their misuse of their freedom, we cannot make the same supposition of the animals. This feeding of animal on animal appears to be their natural way of living and part of the structure of creation. How is *that* to be reconciled with a loving God?

We must bear in mind two points already made. Pain in animals, like pain in men, can't be added up. The greatest pain ever endured in the animal kingdom was the pain of the *one* creature who suffered most. No animal ever endured two animals' pains. We must remember, also, that only the very highest animals have a nervous system like our own, and none has our imagination or anticipation. To "transfer" our pains to the animals, therefore, is foolish. Nonetheless, the problem presented to us here is hard and ugly and no light words can wipe it away.

There is some evidence in the Bible that the origin of evil in the world is older than our race; that there are free beings in the moral universe of a higher order than men and women; that some of these beings gladly and swiftly serve the God who made them and others are in revolt against him. Paul refers to these latter as "principalities" and "powers of darkness" (Eph. 6:12). Not only has man been tempted to misuse his freedom by these evil powers, but disease, and strife, and internal warfare of man and beast may have come this same way. Certainly, Paul binds together the whole creation in its throbbing pain with the purpose of God to save men and women who are deeply sorry for their wrongdoing and turn to him for his forgiveness and help (Rom. 8:18-23).

But here also we walk without complete understanding, and lean on the love we have learned of in other ways.

64

Do We Know Enough to Trust?

MOST PEOPLE USE, AT SOME TIME OR OTHER, "THE LAW OF THE necessary minimum." I mean this: if a sensible fellow is buying a secondhand car, he doesn't concentrate on the size of the trunk, or the quality of the paintwork, or even on whether it has two or four doors; he makes sure about the engine, the brakes, and the tires. If a sensible man's daughter wants to be engaged, the father isn't chiefly concerned (though the girl may be) as to whether the young man is tall and dark and handsome; his concern is about the young man's character. We fix on essentials. We can't know everything, but we ask if we know enough to be reasonably sure.

It is not very different when we look at this mysterious world. No one examining the physical world by itself could conclude that it was obviously made by a good God. The jungle is neutral. Evidence clashes with evidence. Indeed, all the arguments for the existence of God seem to break even, and we have the choice of living under a question mark, denying the existence of God and any deep meaning in life, or making the venture of faith and testing the evidence by prayer, worship, Bible study, and Christian fellowship.

Those of us who have taken this third way are sure that we are right. We have found our faith confirmed. Most are quite sure, and the rest are almost sure, that they are in touch with another. He is good, loving, forgiving, wise.

With this conviction in our minds, we come back to this

mysterious world. The jungle is still neutral. We do not have all the answers, though light falls here and there where before it was quite dark. Do we know enough to trust?

We do know enough to trust. There are problems of pain and providence we cannot fully solve, but we have had enough evidence of God's love to trust. We have seen him in Jesus Christ. We are putting our hand in his and going forward unafraid.

If this is irrational, then every child in the world is irrational too. All children are preplexed at times by their parents. "Why this? Why that?" They are old enough to ask the questions, though not yet old enough to understand the answers. But they trust their father's love.

That is what we are doing.

THE CHURCH

65

Why Is There a Church at All?

BECAUSE CHRIST FOUNDED IT. DELIBERATELY SO. HE SAID, "ON THIS rock I will build my Church." The Church was not the idea or invention of the disciples—as though they said after Christ's death, "Let's have a 'get-together'!" It was founded of set purpose by Christ himself and is, therefore (so Christians believe), a divine institution.

Without claiming to understand all that Christ had in mind when founding the Church, we at least can see some things. Life is not *purely* private and individual. Life *is* personal, but that involves relationships and social life also. How much of a man's life is left, if you take out what he is as son, brother, husband, father, friend, workman, and citizen? We are social beings. Religion isn't only what you are "on your own."

The fullness of the Christian life cannot be known except in fellowship—fellowship with God and fellowship with one another. Moreover, the purposes of God in this world require a social organism by which to express themselves. Far as the Church has fallen below the intention of her divine founder, she is still his best instrument in this world for doing his will.

No one knows better than the leaders and members of the Church how unworthy their witness is, but they know, even in their failure, that it is part of their task to offer the world a picture of what the world might be if it sincerely tried to do the will of God. The Church deplores her divisions, but her different branches are less and less in rivalry with one another, and

QUESTIONS PEOPLE ASK ABOUT RELIGION

love and understanding leap over the barriers which still remain. Christ's intention that his Church should be one, and a great example in the world will yet be realized.

And, if the nations were as near and as sincerely respectful to one another, as the branches of the Church now are, it would be a different world.

66

Can't I Be a Christian and Not a Member of the Church?

IF A MAN LOVED CHRIST AS THE SON OF GOD, IF HE ORDERED HIS life on the example which Christ gave, if he, also, "went about doing good," no one would want to deny, that he was a Christian when he claimed the title himself, and a member of the invisible Church. Yet frankness compels us to say that it would be a limited Christian life that he would enjoy if he were not a member of the *visible* Church.

He would not be acknowledging his debt to the Church in time past. It was through the Church (under God) that he got the Bible. The Church has carried the faith to him through the long centuries. It is hard to see how he could ever have become a Christian at all but for the existence and fidelity of the Church.

He would be failing, also, in many of his Christian duties in the present time. The Church has to give a corporate witness to the Christian life in the nation—and he would have no part in that. The Church has a concern over social justice at home and missionary endeavor abroad, but what orphanage could he open *alone*, and how many missionaries could he send overseas? If he said he had no interest in either of these endeavors, he would be confessing at once to a limit in his Christian concern.

He would be limiting, moreover, his own Christian growth. He would be cut off from the grace of which comes through the sacraments, worship, and Christian fellowship. God has as many avenues to a man's mind as the man has friends who are friends of God; but, if he is trying to be a Christian in isolation, he makes it more difficult for God to help him.

Men who have been imprisoned have maintained their faith in solitary confinement by prayer alone; but almost always they were in the Church in their heart and intention, and usually the Church was aware of their need and was holding them up.

In some watered-down sense of the word a man could be a "Christian" and not a member of the visible Church, but why have skimmed milk when you could have full cream?

67

The Church Is Divided. Which Part Do I Believe?

THE CHURCH IS DIVIDED, BUT LET US BE CAREFUL NOT TO EXAGgerate the divisions. Beneath the divisions which unhappily separate us a present there is a deep underlying unity far stronger than the things which keep us apart. All the major sections of Christendom hold the same classic creeds; almost all of them recognize the validity of each others' baptism; even those which seem most exclusive are less so on examination—the Roman Catholics conceding that sincere Christians in other communions are "Catholic" without knowing it, and Plymouth Brethren allowing that far more are in the true Church of Christ than anyone on earth is aware.

Nevertheless, the divisions in the Church remain a sad contradiction of her reconciling mission in the world, and to see an

Episcopal, a Roman Catholic, and a Baptist standing within a hundred yards of one another, and without any real fellowship between them, weakens the Church's witness and provides an easy excuse for unbelievers to turn a deaf ear to the call of God.

History and temperament must both be borne in mind in seeking to assess the importance of Church differences. People lived before us, and it isn't hard to see how (in matters of belief) honest people could make a different interpretation of Bible teaching, and how (in forms of worship) one man can best approach the Deity with puritanical plainness and another with stately ritual. Some of the differences, of course, are far deeper than this, and are not to be reconciled by calling them two aspects of one truth. On some things, if one group of Christians is right, the others are wrong, but the closer commerce between denominations in recent years has greatly enlarged understanding, and there is a longing eagerness to appreciate the witness which other Christians bear. It may be said with some confidence that Church divisions are a temporary phase. While modes of worship may always vary and methods of Church government may vary too, an enlarging love will prevent one group of believers from denying to other believers a place in the Church that Christ came to found.

Why not join that branch of the Church which (so far as you can judge) most clearly proclaims the truth of Christ by word and life? Yet, having joined, work for the unity of the Church as a whole.

68

What Has the Church Done in the World?

NOT ALL IT SHOULD HAVE DONE, NO DOUBT, BUT MORE THAN ITS opponents admit.

Most of it belongs to the world of values—the real worth of things, and supremely the worth of men and women. But let us examine just one practical point. Consider the Church's care through nearly two thousand years of the sick, the dying, the aged, the orphan, the cripple, the unmarried mother, and the unwanted child.

I once made a journey round the world. I never once saw "The Atheists' Home for Orphans" or "The Agnostics' Crippleage," but everywhere I went I saw the Christian Church caring for the destitute and needy.

Don't misunderstand me! I know individual agnostics and atheists who are compassionate and generous, and no doubt they have their glad share in subscriptions to good causes. But the world's need is barely touched in that way. People must give *themselves*, and give themselves utterly, if the fringe of this vast need is to be touched.

Thousands of Christian folk gladly give themselves to this work. Doctors, nurses, teachers—give up home and its comforts, their career and its advancement, and spend their whole lives in obscure places, and sometimes in appalling conditions, for the love of Christ and their fellow men. They may never return —or return only in old age to live on a pittance at home.

When this was gently pointed out to a militant unbeliever, and the absence of any comparable effort on the part of his associates made clear, he defended himself on the ground that there "weren't so many unbelievers as Christians" and "they hadn't got going yet." Yet only the moment before he had claimed that millions and millions of people shared his views, and that "intelligent" folk had "seen through" Christianity for centuries.

Where does this deep compassion and willingness to sacrifice come from? No slick psychological explanation will do here.

This is the love of God flowing through human hearts. For all her failures, the Christian Church hasn't failed here.

69

Why Is the Church Not More Powerful in the World?

FOR TWO REASONS CHIEFLY—THE WEAKNESS AND EVIL IN MEN, AND the failure of the Church to live up to her divine mission. Let us look at each of them in turn.

Christianity is not an easy creed. It curbs some of the strongest demands of human nature. Based on the Ten Commandments, it insists on the sanctity of truth (though the temptation to lie on occasion is so powerful); it is firm on the difference between "mine" and "thine"; it requires abstinence in sex relationships before marriage and loyalty afterwards. And this is but the beginning. It says we must love our neighbor as ourselves. It would almost unpick our nature and remake us on the model of Christ. It stresses the sacraments, prayer, worship, Bible study, and Christian fellowship. And while these are a joy to people who are inside, they appear as an intolerable burden to those who are not. It is no wonder that men hesitate before the challenge of the Church.

Nor has the Church offered the example to the world which she should have done. Her own history is stained. In ages past, evil men have come to high position in the Church. In some centuries, instead of the Church invading the world to win it for Christ, the world invaded the Church and evil was nourished inside it. The Church, which had so bravely endured persecution, wickedly inflicted it on others. The Church was split and split again, and men have come to love their divisions.

It is no wonder that a divided-Church has no power to heal the divisions of the world.

Yet the Church has always had her saints and Christ has never left it. Perhaps only a divine institution could have survived the double strain of outside pressure and internal strife. The Church is drawing together again. It is one of the lovely facts of this age. Affection leaps over denominational boundaries. More and more people are learning to love the Church in its wholeness and not just their branch of it. A vast volume of prayer arises in every section that God will make his people one.

MISCELLANEOUS

70

Can't I Be Happy Without Doing Right?

No. NOT DEEPLY HAPPY. GOD DID NOT MAKE US TO BE HAPPY AT any price, and good if we could manage it. He made us to be good—and deeply happy as a consequence.

Don't confuse this with priggishness. I am not describing people who feel morally superior to others and are proud because of it. That is probably the most detestable of sins and led Christ to say some of the severest things which ever fell from his lips.

The full answer to the question of whether we can be happy without doing right runs down to those deeper layers of our nature which we noticed when we were considering our basic intuitions. We always knew, we said, that it was right to do right, that kindness was better than cruelty and the truth than a lie.

If these things are basic to our human nature—however much they may be overlaid by our habit of lying to ourselves when we want something which our conscience disapproves—how can we hope to be happy if we are deliberately running against them?

We can be happy *for a time*. We can ignore the disapproval inside us. We can do the very things our moral sense warns us against (in order to silence it if we can), but we can't be deeply and constantly happy. When we are alone, the inner voice awakes again in disapproval, and although it weakens with years of neglect, it is doubtful if it is ever completely silenced. Always it speaks at any rate of the decencies, and there is the power of authority in what it says.

But this has really brought us to the nature of our conscience and we ought to look at that.

71

What Is Conscience?

CONSCIENCE HAS SOMETIMES BEEN CALLED "THE VOICE OF GOD," and while the definition is by no means silly, it is capable of misunderstanding. I once overheard two young mothers talking on the same day about the vaccination of their respective babies. One said, "I *must* get it done. It is on my conscience." The other said, "I am not having it done. It is against my conscience." They were really using the word "conscience" to mean "judgment." In any case, God doesn't speak with two voices.

All men and women have a moral sense. They know what the word "ought" means. "Ought" is *quite* different from "I want," or "it suits my game," or "it is the custom," or "it would be wise." It can be opposed to all these things and still be *commanding*. "*I ought*" is different and universal. People who deny the existence of God have it. I knew a man who always made fun of religion. But he did once (what was unusual for him) a dirty trick, and his *remorse* was terrible. He felt polluted and unclean.

People who disbelieve in God trace this moral sense to what society has found convenient, and it is made impressive (they think) because "our group" is behind it, and it was built into us in childhood.

But this is not deep enough. The sense of shame and pollution which we feel when we run contrary to a sensitive conscience requires more explanation than social convenience. We don't really feel that we *made* the moral order; we became *aware* of it. Nor is it true to say that all morals vary according to the tribe or race. *Some* things vary; but the agreements on the major matters are widespread and striking.

People who deny the existence of God sometimes admit that there *may* be a "moral order," though they leave it hanging in the air and quite unexplained. Those who believe in God find the origin of the moral order in the divine mind.

Nonetheless, we must remember that the moral sense requires education, and Christians believe that the best way to educate it is to think much on the God revealed by Jesus Christ, to talk and listen to him, to worship, and to read with understanding the book in which his unfolding purpose has been made plain.

72

Isn't It Best to Leave Children to Form Their Own Ideas About Religion When They Grow Up?

PEOPLE MEAN ONE OF TWO THINGS WHEN THEY SAY THIS. SOME mean that, while they will be careful to instruct their children in the Christian faith, and "bed them down" therefore in some branch of the Christian Church, they will be careful not to make them little bigots and let them suppose that Christians in other branches of the Church are quite wrong. If, when they are grown, the children find their spiritual home in another section of the Christian family, they will not mind. That is an understandable position.

But it is not the usual one with people who ask this question.

They mean to give their children no religious instruction at all. Some of them are not careful to give the children definite *moral* instruction either. All through the formative years of childhood —when children ask questions (as of course they will)—they are put off with vague answers and grow up in a spiritual haze. The idea appears to be that, when they reach their teens, these uninstructed children will be able to line up in their minds the great spiritual and moral teachers of the world and say to the one they select, "I'll have you." *As if they could!* And as if (not being deeply impressed with the importance of these things) they will even *want* to!

Children have a right to the best that we have learned in every branch of life; in art, music, science, civics—and in religion too. The best this world knows in religion centers in Jesus Christ. To deprive children of instruction in his life and teaching is to rob them of something enormously precious, and if you put nothing in its place, you leave them without a sense of reverence and final authority (which are far more important than we realize) and with no signposts in the moral maze of this world.

And don't deceive yourself that, if you are careful not to give the children any "spiritual" ideas, they won't get any. They may make their own—or borrow bad ones! They may think the world exists just for their enjoyment, and the deep selfishness which is in us all may make them quite repulsive and impossible to live with.

73

Isn't It Enough Just to Encourage the Social Instincts of Children?

PEOPLE WHO DENY THE EXISTENCE OF GOD, BUT FEEL THE IM-portance of morals, say that morality can be built in children's minds quite securely on their social instincts. We should teach them that all people have selfish instincts and social instincts, and that the art of life is to keep these instincts nicely balanced. When we are tempted to do wrong we should say to ourselves, "I must remember my social instincts. Other people must be considered too." And then we shall do the right.

I sometimes wonder if these people know what real temptation is; whether they have ever been in a desperate jam, with careful lying as the only way out; or been in awful need of money, and had to fight night and day a neat little scheme which the subsconscious mind has "cooked-up" ("and of course I can pay it all back later on") ; or have ever known flaming lust, with fierce appetite and easy opportunity arriving together.

The idea of a tempted man in a desperate hour sitting down and saying to himself, "Now, now, I must remember my social instincts," borders on the ludicrous. In such an hour, the social instincts themselves can grease the slope to moral shipwreck. A painted harlot, for example, specializes in sociability. How can it do *her* any harm? It's what she wants.

But if a man believes that the Ten Commandments were given by God and that the Creator has all the right there is to lay down the rules of life, if that man can sense, moreover, behind the Commandments, the strong compassionate figure of Christ and hear him say, "Let me help you here," that man can win through. He may not do it, even then, without "blood and sweat and toil and tears," but his chances are multiplied immeasurably. Those of us who know Christ know this: that the very *thought* of him is cleansing, and to live with him in our mind and heart is to have a steady victory over temptation.

Isn't It Wrong to Call Ourselves "Miserable Sinners"?

CERTAINLY—IF YOU DON'T MEAN IT. BUT WHAT MAKES YOU SO sure that you are not a miserable sinner? Is it the word "miserable" that you object to, or the word "sinner"?

"Miserable" simply means "worthy of pity." But let us leave the word "miserable" aside. Some people continue to be cheerful sinners, and others, who have quite a high opinion of their moral selves, are often miserable. Let us just ask if we are *"sinners"* or not.

The word "sin" is variously used. Some religious people use "sin" just for sex offences, drunkenness, gambling, and playing games on Sunday. Clearly, that definition is too narrow—and biased in their own favor! What of pride, bigotry, cruelty, dubious business deals, evil gossip, and a hard and unforgiving spirit?

But (as we have noticed before) the chief thing wrong with men and women is not this thing or that thing, but their awful self-centeredness. It is true of all people, until deep religion does something for them. "Nice manners" can't alter it; they are a device for covering it up. People are saved (we said) when the center of their life moves from self to Christ. Then they receive supernatural help to live for others, and a divine kindness flows through them which helps everyone they meet.

People with spiritual passion want that more than they want anything. If they could have Christ living in them, every other good thing would follow from it. Without him at the center of their life, they honestly feel that they are sinners (even if they are neighborly and do plenty of "good turns") because their

basic disease has not been cured. Self is first, and they always
have their eye on the "main chance."

"Well—we can't help that," some people protest. "We are
made that way. That is human nature." True enough. But if
we can't do something about human nature, we are finished.
The mess the world is in is only the selfishness of human nature
magnified to the size of nations.

One of the confident claims made for Christ is that he can
change human nature; but before a man is ready to be changed,
he must recognize and admit that he is a sinner and *needs*
changing.

75

Do I Need the Help
of Christ to Be Unselfish?

SOME PEOPLE WOULD SAY "NO." WE ARE MADE UP, THEY ARGUE, OF
selfish and unselfish impulses, and both are equally natural.
They say that we can see this in the animals. Tigers and gorillas
look after their young. Chimpanzees feel sympathetic towards
other sick members of their family. When Christian people say
that they would be utterly selfish but for the influence of Christ,
these critics laugh and reply, "Not so. Your social impulses
would work like other people's. Look at us. We care for *our*
children and friends. You don't need Christ to make you kind."

But this argument has become blurred. Christian don't argue
that it is only their Christianity which makes them kind to their
children and old *parents* (though, even then, they think that it
enlarges and enriches their love). Concern for other members
of one's family (they would say) is only selfishness "once re-
moved." After all, they are *your* children and *your* parents.

108

The claim of Christians is that the love of Christ puts a concern in human hearts for people *not* in their own family, not in their own "set," not even in their own nation. One of the first private proofs that any man or woman has that they have committed their life to Christ is an aching love for other people, for *all* people—a sense of pitiful concern and kinship for the human race. That is how the orphanages, crippleages, and rescue homes arise. That is why thousands go abroad (doctors, nurses, teachers, etc.) for a whole long life of hard and ill-rewarded missionary services.

The opponents of Christianity say that, if we are unselfish to people outside our own circle, the desire for public approval is usually behind it (self again!). But I have never noticed much public approval of missionaries. Their own friends have held them up, but the members of the "public" (having little or no religious conviction themselves) have looked upon missionary work as waste, or interference with other people, or the occupation of cranks. Yet it has been, in its small but lovely way, the most disinterested service rendered by the privileged to the underprivileged countries for generations, and it would never have come out of our social impulses alone. It takes the love of Christ to engender so wide and strong a quality of unselfishness as this.

76

Hasn't Much Good Been Done by Unbelievers?

UNDOUBTEDLY. IT IS A PITY THAT CHRISTIANS HAVE NOT ALWAYS realized and acknowledged it. Some men and women who doubted or denied the existence of God have been leaders in social reform and splendidly generous in the service of their fellow men.

Some unbelievers have served us, also, in bravely challenging the bigotry of other days, and have had their honorable share in securing the freedom of thought we all now enjoy. The Christians who fought slavery had among their finest colleagues men who denied God's existence but who were busy on God's work.

Yet it is interesting to note how often these people came out of Christian homes. I once made a study of the lives of these men and women with that point particularly in mind. Almost without exception they had had the advantage of a Christian upbringing.

The two facts are not unconnected; their high regard for morals, their passion for social progress, their hatred of injustice and wrong sprang from the religion they had come to reject. They often failed to recognize the connection themselves, but what had been built into their character in childhood came to fruition in maturity.

A traveler once came upon a tribe of people who were moon worshipers. He expressed some surprise at their preference and said that he would have expected them to worship the sun. "But why?" they inquired. "The sun foolishly shines in the day time when there is plenty of light. The moon conveniently shines at night when it's dark!"

They did not know, either, that the moon was borrowing its light from the sun! Militant unbelievers sometimes multiply in their imagination the social service of those who share their views (and Christians must be careful not to *minimize* it), but even so, it is usually a borrowed light. Their moral zeal derives from the religion they have now tossed aside.

Aren't Some Religious People Quite Repulsive?

SOME ARE! NOT MANY, PROPORTIONATELY. AND IT IS MODEST, OF course, whenever we find other people repulsive, to wonder if they find us repulsive too.

But it cannot be doubted that there *are* religious people from whom other people recoil, and it is not without interest to inquire how this occurs. Some religious people are particularly bitter and abusive in controversy—controversy with unbelievers, and even with their fellow Christians who may differ with them in theology or Biblical interpretation. People who oppose all religion say that this bitterness arises from the weakness of their arguments and proves their irrationality. As a religious writer I often get similarly bitter and abusive letters from militant atheists, so no doubt it works both ways. But the so-called "Christians" would still come under the greater condemnation. They profess to follow a Lord of love, and the militant atheist gives the best jeers of his life to destroy the very idea of a Deity.

Other people who make the Christian faith unattractive do so by giving their message a twist. Ignoring the fact that the Bible offers us a *growing* revelation of God, they quote its high authority to defend policies and practices entirely out of harmony with the mind of Christ. Polygamy, slavery, racial separation, and hatred, could all be defended with high names from the Old Testament. There are sects which claim to be Christian and teach an almost barbaric idea of God.

Bad religion is a peculiarly evil thing. There is in the very nature of strong religion so deep a devotion, and dynamic, and undeviating pursuit of what is held to be right, that if this is

111

misdirected, the most tragic consequences will follow. Chris
seeks to guard his servants from this awful danger by requir
ing that their devotion to what they understand as truth shal
never rob them of love for those who oppose them or differ with
them. It is part of the tragedy of Christianity that some of those
who profess it fail here, and make the faith they would com-
mend seem repulsive to people who might have been won by a
bit of sincere love.

But people who decline to consider the claims of Christ because some Christians are repulsive are still missing the best of
all.

78

Why Couldn't the Universe Have "Just Happened"?

A MAN MUST SETTLE THIS QUESTION FOR HIMSELF. IT COMES OUT
of the very inside of him. It doesn't depend on how much
science he knows (because it is a question which science can't
settle, and in any case eminent men in all branches of science
are convinced of God), and in some senses it doesn't depend on
how much he knows *about* God. I say *about* God. There are at
least two ways of knowing. We can know by hearsay, and we can
know by personal experience. I know by hearsay that there are
people on the little island of Tristan da Cunha though I've
never been there, but that knowledge is very different from the
knowledge I had of my father, to whom I talked every day
through my boyhood, on whose strength I leaned, and whom I
knew for *myself*.

People with a personal experience of God don't know *about*

112

God; they know *God*. They don't feel dependent on this or that argument because they have private reasons for being sure. Yet (as we have conceded already) these private reasons can't be given away, and a man without that experience may feel that he knows only *about* God. What answer has *he* to the statement of unbelievers that the universe "just happened"?

He must go (I say) inside himself. Uninfluenced, at the moment, by those who argue for or against a Creator, let him look at the world. He sees purposefulness everywhere—in the lower forms of life and in the higher, in birds, beasts, fish, and men. Governed by what we call "instinctive intelligence" all creatures preserve their life, mate, make a home, care for their young. There is purpose everywhere. In man it flowers. His amazing mind is now probing outer space, and he plans to land on the moon.

If there is a recognized purpose in the parts, is there none in the *whole*? Is it credible that all this came by blind chance? Is it fully rational to suppose that the mind of man is the highest mind in the universe? Did unreason produce reason?

That is what a man must settle for himself. I am with those who say, "It *couldn't* have 'just happened.' "

79

What Is This I Hear About Continuous Creation?

ASTRONOMERS BELIEVED AT ONE TIME (AND SOME STILL DO) THAT creation began in time, and they even made estimates as to when the universe was made. Opinion is now moving to the view that the universe never had a beginning and will never have an end, that there is no limit to time or space, and that creation is ceaseless and continuous process. If certain experiments which are planned confirm this guess, it is confidently predicted by some astronomers that the idea of God will be banished forever from the minds of rational men.

The argument is interesting for many reasons. When Christians argued that God was a being without beginning and without end their opponents ridiculed the idea on the ground that Being without beginning and without end was quite inconceivable. It now appears that a universe without beginning and without end is not only conceivable, but about to be proved. When Christians argued that God was the prime cause of a creation and had made all things, people opposed to the idea of God often exclaimed, "But who made God?" and felt that they had finished their opponents off. Now that a universe "without beginning" is being offered to thoughtful men and women, are the roles reversed and is it the Christian's turn to say in this new accent, "But who made the universe?"

The new aspect of the great debate does not seem so very different from the old. The medical student who, after a few weeks in the dissecting room, announced that he had disposed of God and religion forever because, having minutely examined the human body, he could find no trace of a soul, is not so different from the astronomers. Their telescopes have probed into space, but because they have not brought God into clear focus some of them say that he does not exist. Where is the evidence? His being does not yield to that kind of instrument. It is still pertinent to ask, "If creation is continuous, who is continually creating?" The belief in creation by God does not necessarily mean an instantaneous, complete creation. Is it not still sensible to inquire, "Did the chance action of element on element produce man, mind, the astronomer, and the saint?"

A wise man once said, "Two rows of bricks in a desert proves primitive man. The whole universe proves nothing."

80

Is Fear the Basis of All Religion?

SOME PEOPLE THINK SO. THEY THINK THAT FEAR OF THE unknown led men to "invent" a kind Father above; fear of death led them to dream of everlasting life; fear of punishment led them to try to "make up" to the gods. It was all fear (they say), and because there is nothing in the fear there is no need for the remedy.

Man's first dim awareness of God filled him with awe—and awe includes an element of fear. Man felt a fascination which drew him, and a dread which half stopped him. It may be that fear of the unknown and fear of God's just anger both had their place in the mind of early man.

But fear is not always a bad thing. We can notice today that some forms of fear are fine and fruitful. Fear of an accident is still the best safety "device" on our overcrowded streets. Fear of a dread disease kept many men "moral" in the war. The motive may not have been high, but it was a help to tempted man. Fear of the dark invented the candle, the lamp, the electric light. Fear of sickness is a constant spur to research.

If an element of fear mingled with man's first approach to the Deity, that need neither surprise nor disturb us; but the suggestion that religion is simply the fruit of the crude fears set out in the first paragraph oversimplifies the origins and allows nothing at all for the growth in man's higher understanding of God.

The world is still there—and we have found it impossible to accept the idea that it "just happened." Our moral sense is still there—and we have found it impossible to accept the idea that it is just the fruit of what society has found convenient. And the more we advance in Christian experience (without losing anything of our sense of awe) the more and more our religion centers in love—the love of God, and the love of our fellow men.

Fear as the explanation of it all is too shallow for acceptance.

81

Hasn't Religion Filled People's Minds with Fear?

SOME RELIGION HAS. WE NOTICED IN ANSWERING THE LAST QUESTION that man's first dim awareness of God filled him with awe, and that awe includes an element of fear. Primitive man feared the gods because of the awful punishments they might inflict on the whole tribe, and early laws for the same reason were often especially severe on anything felt to be offensive to the deities.

But it isn't only primitive religion which is charged with filling people's minds with fear. The religion of today—and the Christian religion especially—is said to fall under this condemnation. People are threatened with awful punishment in this life, and the next, if they do not keep the religious code, and the minds of little children have these damaging dreads built into them from their tenderest years. Indeed, some psychiatrists complain that certain of their patients have become nervous wrecks because they were taught as children that sexual promiscuity was wrong. If promiscuity is not to be encouraged, they say, let us be clear that a little license won't do any harm!

We must be frank about this. No doubt some religious people

have been guilty of misusing fear. Some do *still*. They have often attached, in their minds and in their teaching, the severest penalties to the most trifling deeds. Some of us can remember getting the impression that the wrath of God would fall upon us if we used a bus on a Sunday!

But to brush aside the whole ministry of fear by absurdities like this is foolish and dangerous. There is a high moral code, given by God, and confirmed in our conscience, which we ought to fear to break. Sin is sin, and the feeling of guilt acknowledges it. The Church claims to teach us what we should fear. Not all fear (as we have just noticed) is bad, but many fears which haunt the minds of men and women are fitting fears, and yet can be swept out by the Christian faith. God is willing to forgive sin if we are sincerely repentant—and only *God* can forgive sin. The Christian faith removes more fear than it fosters.

It remains true that it *is* a fearful thing to oppose the living God, and a fearful thing also to miss fullness of life here, and in the world to come.

82

Does It Matter if Religion Isn't True, So Long as It Is Useful?

SOME PEOPLE MAKE A DEFENSE OF RELIGION, NOT ON THE GROUND that it is true, but on the ground that it is useful. It is not always easy to understand their minds. Some of them appear to be convinced unbelievers. Some of them are not sure where they stand. But both are disposed to brush aside the question of truth, and to argue that, if religion does people good (or they think it does them good), let them have it. Perhaps it *is* a buttress to morality. If the thing is useful, why bother, whether or not it is true?

Christian people are not grateful for this spurious defense of their faith. That religion *is* a buttress to morality they are in no doubt at all. But the living God is not to be vaporized into some impersonal power which "makes for righteousness." He is *The Power* who makes for righteousness and from whom all precious things (for individuals and communities) flow. To deny his being, while you clutch at one of his fancied effects, is trafficking with truth.

This same word needs to be said to the people who say that "religion might be true for some people but isn't true for *them!*" If they mean that some people have an experience of God and are sure of him (though they haven't and they aren't), their position is understandable, but if they are suggesting that the reality of the universe is affected by human opinion, it is nonsense.

God *is*—whether you believe in him or not. The great Being behind the universe does not depend for his existence on mortal minds. The supposition that, if you dismiss the idea of God from your thought you dismiss God, is surely the apex of human vanity.

The one grain of truth embedded in this muddled thinking is the truth we have stressed before in these pages. We cannot be sure of religion without committal. Religion will never be real to you if you stand outside it. It can be known only from within. Refuse to venture and you have settled *not* to know.

Does God Really Require
That We Worship Him?

IN THE FIRST WEEK THAT I WAS IN THE ARMY, I SPOKE TO A SER-geant-major and didn't call him "Sir." He was very angry. Thrusting his cuff (which bore the mark of his rank) under my nose, he said, "What's that?" "It is a crown," I murmured. "And what does it mean?" he demanded. "It means," I said, "that you are a company sergeant-major." "Yes," he hissed, "and it means, also, that when you speak to me you must say 'Sir.'"

There are some misguided people who suppose that God is like a colossal sergeant-major, that he *demands* worship because he enjoys it, that he watches jealously to see how many people go to church on Sunday to praise him, and is swift to punish those who don't, that he is touchy about the amount of adoration he receives.

God is not like that. It borders on the blasphemous to distort the truth of things and make a caricature of the holy God. Christians worship because they *must*. They have seen God in Jesus Christ. They are convinced that the great being who made the universe (and is far too great to be fully understood) can yet be "sensed," known, spoken to, loved.

The more his wonder breaks on their minds, the more do Christians worship him—so remote yet so accessible, so holy yet so merciful, so wise and yet so loving too. Adoration leaps out of their hearts because it will. It would be as reasonable to expect them *not* to praise him as to expect any honest lover to choke back the expression of his love. If any man feels no impulse to worship, it can be only because he has caught no glimpse of the living God.

Nor is it hard to see the gains of this to men and women.

To know what and who is "tops" (as the children say) in this universe is most important; millions live with a vague sense of "emptiness" over them because they lack all sense of touch with God. To know what is of real "worth" in this world, and kneel to it, draws you up to the best. Moreover, it keeps you in your own little place. It is part of the vanity of men and women to exaggerate their importance. It is spiritually healthy for proud mortals to get down on their knees. If God desires worship from us, it is still for *our* good.

84

If We Know God, Do We Have the Answer to All Things?

BY NO MEANS. IT WAS PLAIN, WHEN WE FACED THE PROBLEMS listed under "Providence," that we had not a full answer to many things. We have *insight*. Some light falls for us on the dark road, but we cannot clear up the problems of cancer, or why one type of animal feeds on another, or why there are "faults" in the earth's surface—or many other things either.

It is foolish to pretend that we can. As we have said before, the most devout Christians have areas of reverent agnosticism in their minds, and to suggest that we have "all the answers" is false and vain. The Bible never claims to answer every question any man might ask. It claims to be a "lamp to our feet"—that is, to give enough light to show a path through this dim world.

What Christians claim in "Christian experience" is not to pick up a body of wrought-out knowledge on the cheap, and to have a pat reply to all the mysteries of the universe, but to be aware of a Presence. It does not come to the average Christian by visions of rapture (though some rare souls *do* enjoy these experiences too); it comes normally by prayer and worship. As the Christian responds to the Presence and ventures forward, he becomes acquainted with a person—holy, loving, and merciful, and one who proves his personal care over all who turn to him in trust.

It is being sure of God and his nature which enables Christians to be sanguine in the face of ugly problems they cannot solve. If God is there and God is love, all must ultimately be well; there *must* be an answer to these mysteries, even though it eludes us at present. To be sure of God is *not* to have the answer to all things, but to be sure that we *shall* have it some day, and that, when we have it, we shall see that it was woven with wisdom and with love.

85

Why Is There So Much "You Must Trust" in Religion?

IT ISN'T IN RELIGION ONLY. SOME OF THE MOST LOVELY THINGS in life would be spoiled if trust were taken away and a doubting mind demanded proof where no proof could be given.

Imagine a couple on the eve of their wedding. Suppose the bride picks up an evening paper and reads a report of the latest batch of broken marriages.

All these people (she reflects) thought that they were in love once, and now they are dragging their romance through the divorce court. How sordid and repulsive it seems!

A doubt comes into her mind. Will *her* marriage end up this way? Why should *she* be an exception to what threatens to become a rule? She turns to her bridegroom and says, "How do I know that you will always love me? *Prove* it to me."

What can the poor fellow do? He may say, "We've known each other for for five years. I've always been true. *Of course* I love you. I'd do anything in the world for you that I could."

Yet she persists. She says, "*Prove* it to me. Prove it to me for the future—when I'm old and grey and ill."

What *can* he do? He will have to say, "You must trust me. I am worthy of your trust. Whatever happens, I will be true. The years will prove it." But now a doubt intrudes into *his* mind. What is wrong with the girl, he wonders. She wouldn't keep saying "Prove it to me" if she wasn't doubting herself. So she doubts *him!* There is hurt in that. Trust is lovelier than proof. Proof compels. Trust confides. Trust may seem less sure than proof, but it is more beautiful, because it doesn't need proof. Proof isn't better than trust in the tenderest relationships. It isn't so good.

God says, "Trust me. I don't compel your minds and hearts. You are free to give or withhold your trust and your love. But let us live together. The passing years will bring their own experience of my constancy and, in my own way, I will make you sure."

86

I Reject Religion, but Often Feel the Need of a Supreme Authority. Is That Unusual?

NOT AT ALL. I THINK IT IS FAIRLY COMMON AMONG PEOPLE WHO reject religion, and it deserves, therefore, examination.

The sense of need for a supreme authority awakes in people in different ways. It comes to some from considering the awareness of right and wrong inside them. How different it is at heart from "preference" or "taste" or "custom." As we have seen, "social convenience" is too shallow an explanation of it. Doesn't it point to a supreme authority whose rule it is?

It comes to others as they think of the problem of juvenile delinquency. They have heard of the lad of seventeen who befriended an old lady of eighty to steal her handbag, and who was asked by the magistrate, "Don't you realize that this is wrong?" "That's what *you* think," he answered. Is morality just opinion spread large? Doesn't it require a sanction above what "*I* think" and "*You* think"? The fact that we seem to *require* it wouldn't prove that it is there, but it would point to its high probability.

Some nuclear scientists have felt the need, as they have seen their science turned into bombs. The state requires this service from them, but who or what is the state that it should say the last word on world destruction? They feel that someone above *all* states should say what should happen to this world.

It all points one way. Who or what is behind this world: blind force, a leering devil, or a loving Father? And don't say that it makes no difference to conduct which you choose. Three schoolboys were discussing their headmasters. One said, "We never *see* him. They say he's so busy. He doesn't even come to morning prayers." Another said, "Ours is a beast. He has favorites too, and he gets into frightful tempers." The third said, "Ours is grand. He seems to know us all. He always calls me by my name, and I'm only in the third form." Is this different attitude to the headmaster going to make no difference to the conduct and character of those boys? Of course it will.

If you feel the need for a supreme authority, why not give God a chance to prove to you that he is there?

Isn't Religion Old-fashioned?

I SUPPOSE I COULD ANSWER THIS QUESTION BY SAYING THAT IN some countries, and in some circles, religion is quite the latest vogue. I could enlarge on the undergraduate who said recently, "My parents are quite old-fashioned. They don't believe in God!" But I put that kind of exchange deliberately aside, if only because of the immaturity of thought which lies behind all this confusion between truth and fashion.

If a thing is true, it is true whether it is fashionable or not. Fashion can affect hats, and dress, and types of entertainment, and modes of speech, and social convention, and many other things, but not basic morality, and not the being of God. When God gave the Ten Commandments, he gave them for all time.

It is this which makes so much of the common criticism of religious observance plainly silly. People say sometimes to those of us to whom Sunday is a different day, "How Victorian!" If we are not amused at an obscene joke, they may remark to someone else, "He doesn't live in the modern world." If we don't conceal our conviction that a marriage license is deeply different from a dog license, they say, "He doesn't understand that times have changed."

Let me be plain and say of this question what I have said of no other—that it is silly, that truth is truth—whatever the gossip of the streets may be, and whatever our own personal preferences may be.

T. H. Huxley, when he lost his little child, declined the comfort some friends offered him when they spoke of heaven, because he wasn't convinced that heaven existed. Heaven was a much more "fashionable" belief then than it is now, but this man, so devoted to truth, would not be swayed by fashion.

Splendid! Yet, if the world is only material, why this devotion to truth? (Does matter matter that much?) It illustrates again that the best unbelievers are better than their unbelief. Truth is more than matter, and is unaffected by fashion, and Huxley's brave attitude only makes sense if there is a Being behind the universe to whom a lie is an offense and who requires truth in the men and women whom he has made.

88

Isn't Religion Just a Survival of Superstition?

THIS QUESTION DOES, AT LEAST, ADMIT THAT MAN DIDN'T INVENT God. There are people who believe that the idea of God began in man's intellect, that being afraid of the dark, or death, or his own dreadful loneliness, he "thought-up" a Supreme Being. Man didn't invent God; he became *aware* of him, and the early efforts to approach God among primitive people were crude in the extreme. They began often with a fetish, and later worshiped an idol. God was thought of, at first, as belonging to the tribe, and then the nation. Only slowly did man perceive that the great God must be universal.

God always respects human growth. Man grew in his knowledge of God, as he grew in his knowledge of things. God's eagerness to reveal himself was measured to man's readiness to respond. Man's readiness to respond measured his capacity to receive.

But it isn't the *origin* of things so much as their *end* which explains them. When the wife of the Rector of Epworth, Lincolnshire, told her husband in the autumn of 1702 that they were going to have another child, John Wesley was an unformed fetus in her womb. Only God could know that the spiritual health of the world would be mightily affected by the yeasting life of those half-formed cells. Not what it is in its beginnings, but what it will become in its unfolding, best explains the divine purpose in things.

"Take one swallow's nest, the fat of one young vulture and one goose, the parings of ten fingernails, the juice of one wild cucumber and boil together. Mix a paste of the residue and add one green lizard. Place in a red rag and tie the red rag around the patient's neck." That was the accepted medical prescription for the cure of gout, chills, and fevers six hundred years ago. Will you wipe all medicine aside today because the best doctors of the fourteenth century came at their work in that fashion? Will you refuse to consult the doctor in the twentieth century because the origins of his high skill are more crude even than this fantastic poultice?

Religion among primitive men was crude, superstitious, sometimes even barbaric. But they were dimly aware of God, and God was leading them on.

89

Isn't One Religion as Good as Another?

WELL, IS IT? IN REMOTE PARTS OF AFRICA THERE ARE STILL PRIMI-tive tribes whose religion includes obedience to witch doctors, and the witch doctors can make the people almost crazy with fear, and demand (on occasion) the ceremonial murder of people. Not many generations ago (though Hinduism must not be judged mainly by this) the Hindu widow was burned on the bonfire of her husband's corpse. The idea that one religion is as good as another is usually the fruit of ignorance of the facts, and of unwillingness to face the challenge which religion presents.

Religions can be compared in a serious and scholarly way. Their differences are not to be dismissed merely as "a matter of taste." The ethical heart of them can be tested by widely accepted "standards," and even if there are still matters in sharp dispute, no informed person would say that "one religion is as good as another."

Religions should be compared at their best. To point out the failures of weak individuals to live up to their faith settles nothing, and to blame a religion for the misdeeds of a nation which is not sincerely following the faith whose name it bears is unfair also.

People complain at times that the world wars have both come out of "Christian" countries. They try to smear Christ with the slime of the gas chamber and concentration camp, though these are a plain contradiction of all he taught. It is true, also, that other world faiths are sending missionaries to Christian countries to save the world from the "horrors" of Christianity.

But these are distortions. The great majority of people in Ceylon are Buddhists. A central and noble doctrine of Buddhism is "reverence for life." "Never kill" the people are taught; "under no circumstances must you kill." Yet (with a comparatively small population of less than nine millions) Ceylon exceeds a murder a day. This does not disprove Buddhism. It only proves again that men and women are weak.

What Is the Attitude of Christianity to Other World Faiths?

ONE OF HIGH RESPECT, OF GRATITUDE FOR THE SPIRITUAL INSIGHT of their founders, of honest desire to understand better what they teach, and of sincere recognition of the deep reason why they have fed the spiritual life of their followers through many centuries.

Christians did not always take this attitude to the other world faiths. There was a time when Christians dismissed all non-Christians as "heathen." Because scientific discovery was more advanced in Christian countries, people visiting the East got confused at times between plumbing and spiritual insight, and because Orientals hadn't always a clean water supply they supposed they had no real inkling of the great God. But that has passed. Informed Christians are grateful to the Buddhists (as we have just said) for their teaching on "reverence for life"; the spiritual penetration of the Mohommedan mystics is being more widely recognized, and, as for the Jewish religion—well, Christianity sprang from it and can't be understood apart from it.

Nevertheless, Christians firmly hold that Christ was a visitation of God himself to this world; that although God had spoken by the Eastern sages and Hebrew prophets, he spoke his clearest word in his Son; that although these other great religious teachers were a light to their areas, Christ is the light of the world; and that all that these others had seen of truth is confirmed and fulfilled in him and, where they erred, he puts them right.

Christians desire more fellowship with those who hold these other faiths. They remember with sadness their past contempt.

They want to share what they are convinced is their greatest treasure, and they are sure that, as Christ is better known, he will win all hearts.

91

Is There a Judgment?

THE BIBLE TEACHES THAT THIS LIFE IS NOT THE WHOLE OF LIFE. It is a probation. We are being tested, and judgment, therefore, is involved in it.

Our experience confirms this. Judgment runs through all life. Sometimes we say that things are tested by "life," or by "time," but even in common and vague phrases like these, we are admitting the testing which is in all life. Moreover, the moral sense we all find in ourselves (and which we could not explain away on grounds of social convention) shows us that the judgment to which we are being subjected is a moral one. The awareness of "I ought" (which is in us all) points plainly to goodness, duty, and a law high above "convenience."

In every week we live we are making our characters. Every day brings moral choices for us—some small, some big. By the choices we make (between the right and the wrong, between the lower and the higher good) we are building our character. When the body falls away in death, and we appear on that plane where spiritual values are *seen* as supreme, we are judged. It will be plain (even to ourselves) what we have become.

Although the basic molding of our character is shaped to goodness (for we were made in the image of God), there is now in the bowl a bias which makes evil very attractive to us in some moods and circumstances. Men and women might say with justification that God was unjust, if he had left them without help in this battle against temptation.

But God has not left them without help. The central offer of the Christian message is that God will help any man who turns to him, will forgive his past and strengthen him in his present struggles, and bring him to the judgment humble and unafraid.

92

Is There a Heaven?

THE NEW TESTAMENT IS COMPLETELY POSITIVE UPON THE POINT. We do not just go into the earth and rot. Our real selves, which survive the decay of our bodies, submit to judgment and receive their reward.

But while the New Testament is emphatic on the fact of heaven, it gives us no "guidebook" to it. No one knows the details of life in that realm, and it is almost certainly beyond description in any language of earth. There are other reasons also why it is well that the wonder of heaven should not be in full view. If we could really see the marvel of it, we should lose all taste for life as we have it here. Life loses attraction for the humiliated and heartbroken, and people to whom the wonder of heaven was plain to see would be under enormous temptation at times to make their own way there. So a veil divides us. We see one life at a time.

Yet a careful examination of what the Bible *does* say about heaven makes three things clear. It is a sphere of growth, work, and great happiness.

Heaven is not static. God means to perfect all who come, and he has all eternity in which to do it.

Nor is heaven a place of endless church services—with the

choir doing most of the work! Jesus said. "My Father works even until now, and I work." When John caught a glimpse of heaven in a vision, he said of those he saw there, "They *serve* him day and night."

As for the happiness of heaven—language fails again. The Bible says quite plainly that in heaven there is no evil, no sorrow, and no pain. What it must be to those who love God deeply to be for ever in his presence none can know till they are there. To quote the Bible again, it is "above what we can ask or think."

93

Is There a Hell?

ONE CANNOT READ THE BIBLE AND MISS THE REFERENCES TO HELL. They are in the teaching of Christ himself. Some passages describe it as a place of fire and torment, though not many Christians believe in literal flame. To be in hell is to be out of the presence of God.

If man's freedom is real, he is free to turn from God and persist in the direction he has chosen. If God forces himself on no one (because he respects the freedom which he has given), even those of us most aware of the love of God must concede the possibility that some will resist that love to the last.

Some devout Christians—knowing that there are people in so-called "Christian" countries who have never really felt the impact of God's love—believe that the persuasions of God will persist beyond death, and they nourish the hope that all will ultimately be saved. But most of these admit that there is no plain and quite unmistakable promise in the Bible to that effect, and they know that, if God compelled people to accept him, he would be treating them as "things" and not as persons. Their hope is based on their sense of the power of God's love, and their belief that God will not cease to love the erring while there are other mortals who love them too.

The enormous importance of this life emerges again. Character solidifies. We grow into certain ways and get "set" in them. Some men seem to live only for the body: gorging, swilling, fornicating (ugly words, but they are ugly things) . One wonders what will be left when the body falls away. In their company, spiritual matters are the subject only of obscene jokes. They honestly hate holy things. Heaven would be hell to them.

So let us remember that hell is not a fitting subject for jokes, nor yet to be waived airily aside on the ground that God is a "gentleman" who will overlook everything at the last. He made us free; and we are free, if we choose, to be damned.

94

What Could Christ Do
for an Ordinary Man?

CHRIST CARES FOR ALL MEN WITH AN EQUAL AFFECTION. IF HE can do more through a man with many gifts, it isn't because he loves talented people more, but only because the man has more to offer. Nevertheless, if a man with one talent offers it to Christ, he can be more effective in the best things than a man with five talents who keeps them to himself.

This is what Christ will do for any man who sincerely asks his help:

He will forgive his sins. We all have them. The man who thinks he hasn't any is self-deceived. There is no one living whose conscience will not convict him on something, if he gives his conscience the chance. Your subconscious mind knows this even if your conscious mind doesn't. At the last, no one can be completely happy and completely at peace until he is forgiven.

He will put a sense of purpose in a man's life. Many men over forty wonder what life is *for*. They find it hard to believe that there is a divine purpose being worked out behind things, and (if there is) they don't see where they come in. Christ can meet that need. He can give a man a warm sense of assurance that the world has meaning and that his own little life can be used for great ends.

Consequently, he can make a man know that he is fulfilling himself, that life isn't just "one thing after another," or

QUESTIONS PEOPLE ASK ABOUT RELIGION

even "Come day, go day; God bless Sunday." He can convince him that when a man listens, God speaks, and that this life of ours can be lived under guidance. He will tell him things to do, and work with him in the doing of them.

He will use him to help others. His secret life can be full of quiet service. He can do more "good turns" than he ever did on his own, and they will meet the *deeper* needs of people in a way he was incapable of doing before.

He will give him inward peace, light on the problems of life, and a happiness deeper than anything he ever tasted. Indeed, so great is the contrast between life with Christ and life without him that people who have known both say in simple honesty that they only began to live when they began to live with him.

All this Christ will do for any man. He said, "Him that cometh to me, I will in no wise cast out." (John 6:37.)

95

What Could Christ Do for My Home?

If Christ is recognized as the head of a home, all kinds of lovely things occur in consequence.

Any good home is a refuge from the cares of the world, but with Christ as the head, the sense of refuge is multiplied and a great sense of *renewal* is added as well. One steps through the door into peace and love.

Any good home has love in it, but when Christ is welcomed there, the love is enriched and enlarged. Even in homes where people "get along all right" quarrels occur, and sometimes a fairly frequent bickering. The deep selfishness of our nature makes it inevitable. One wants the TV on when another wants it off. People argue about whose turn it is to do the chores. Nerves get frayed.

Christ has enormous power to affect all these things. If he has been welcomed into every heart, as well as recognized as head of the home, they just don't occur. Everyone has a caring concern about the rest. Nor do people in such a home take each other for granted. In some "nice" homes, months can go by without the expression of any gratitude or affection. (The idea of it may even be dismissed as "sentimental".) In some "nice" homes, every member of the family is an individual. They are living their own lives and resent inquiries from the rest. Home is little more than a parking place and filling station.

Christ alters all that. He knits the family together. He makes confidences easier between children and parents. Children recognize the place of discipline, and parents realize that the children are mentally more mature than they thought. Yet he does not allow the family to become an exclusive clique. Being *his* home, he wants it shared. There are lonely folk to whom an hour at a family fireside would be a bit of heaven.

All this is a consequence of the recognition of Christ as the head of the home. It is harder if only one member of the family recognizes Christ's headship, but even that means that he is *in*. The patience and co-operation of *one* member of the family with Christ could transform the home.

96

What Could Christ Do Where I Work?

THE FIRST THING CHRIST EXPECTS OF HIS SERVANTS IN THEIR PLACE of work is that they be good workmen. Religious people who use the firm's time in prolonged talks on religion with other people are not consistently Christian. The first thing Christ would do for you where you work would be to make you good at your job.

It cannot be doubted that he was good at his own trade. No beast was ever chafed by a yoke which he had made. When he had finished a wooden roof, it didn't leak. Our work isn't something apart from our religion. It is one of the chief ways by which we express it.

Christ's demand for the highest in our work is made equally to all his servants—in housekeeping and bookkeeping, in national and local government, in art and commerce, in business and education, in profession and in unskilled labor, in the office and on the factory floor. Being the rightful Lord of this world, all wholesome work is his.

The task of the Christian at work is a double one. He wants the whole enterprise he is involved in—professional or commercial (whichever it is)—to be done for Christ's sake. He believes that that will give a quality to the work not so likely to come in any other way (if only because it is the "Highest" who calls out our "utmost"). But the Christian also hopes, in the day-to-day contact with the people with whom he works, to be used by Christ for their help, and possibly for their recognition of his claim upon them.

In a large business, and in order to further this double endeavor, Christians need to know each other, and (outside business hours) to get together for prayer and to receive God's direction for their common task. A danger lurks in this. Non-Christians may think them an exclusive clique, with a "holier-than-thou" attitude; so it is all the more important that they should be good at their job and among the kindest people about.

Yet it is beyond all question that Christ has power to transform a business—that men and management, union officials

136

and directors, can so feel his power that dedication comes into daily work, and a man can earn his living to the glory of God.

97

What Could Christ Do for My Town?

CHRIST COULD CHANGE A TOWN AS HE COULD CHANGE A HOME OR business. It is harder and rarer only because there are more people who resist his rule. But it is beyond question with those who know his power that he could do it.

That the life of some towns is so little affected by the Church in its midst is explained in part by the mistaken habit of certain Christian people of living semiexclusive lives. Their home and church take up the whole of their existence. They feel no need to work out the purposes of Christ in their community. Indeed, some of them oppose the very idea of it on the ground that they don't "belong" to this world but to the next. That many of them are sincerely devout is not to be doubted, and it is certain that the town gains something from their prayers and quiet witness, but these are not a maximum for God. Unconsciously, they are failing the one they sincerely want to serve.

I know a town in America which boasted some years ago that it had more people going to church for the size of its population than any other town in the country. Nobody contradicted the claim, though somebody pointed out that the town had another distinction also; it had some of the worst slums in the country too. Nor could *this* be contradicted, and the Church people of the town were ashamed. But they turned their shame into prayer and into action, and they pressed and worked for improvement with such effect that their town has since received a national award for the success of its slum clearance.

Christ is eager to use his Church in private and social service in every community where it exists. Some men eager for social improvement shun the Church because they feel that it does not share their zeal, but they may not know that people who are going to be fully effective in lasting social service have to be themselves remade by Christ—else their natural selfishness will assert itself, and honor, position, or "kudos" may become their unconscious motive.

Yet with changed men and women, sensitive to his whole will, Christ could change *any* town.

98

What Could Christ Do for My Country?

WHEN CHRISTIANS REALIZE THAT CHRIST HAS A MISSION TO COMmunities as well as to the individual, they "raise their sights" and wonder what he could do for their whole land. Inevitably, it depends on the willingness of men and women to accept his rule for their lives, but when this is granted and a sense of his wide strategy is felt, no limit need be put to the sweep of his influence.

The outworking of his will necessarily involves politics. It *must* do. Politics involves *party* politics. Inevitably so—even if the party changes with changing times. Some Christians recoil from this. So much of party politics is pure "party"—petty, childish, unworthy of men set aside for the high affairs of state.

But it is no answer to this littleness for Christians to ignore or abandon politics. It provides all the more reason why men who have suffered the self-crucifixion which dedication to Christ involves, should go into politics—of honest desire that his will shall be done. It will involve them in party allegiance, but not in the party fanaticism which denies that people on the other side can be Christians also. The onward march of God's purposes requires the twin principles of conserving the good and laboring for the better. It is finding the balance of those two principles (worked out in the affairs of day to day) which is the high responsibility of those who make our laws.

Yet it is not *their* responsibility alone. Christian citizenship requires an intelligent interest in these things from all who are servants of Christ and who, in the creation of the public opinion by which alone laws can be made and altered, take their share in drawing this country nearer the intention of Christ.

And in ways *not* obviously political—in social thinking and in social salvage work—the Christian will labor also that Christ may make his country Christian in fact as well as in name.

99

What Could Christ Do for the World?

THE BIBLE TEACHES THAT AT SOME TIME THE WORLD WILL END. IT began in time and it will end in time. Nobody knows when the time will be. Christ himself was unaware of it; he said so himself (Mark 13:32). But this present world order *will* end, and in that day (so the Bible stresses) Christ will be *seen* to be King.

In every generation since the Church was founded there have been Christians who expected the end of the world in their own day. There are some who expect it in this generation. Others believe that the present world order will continue for vast ages beyond our power to foresee.

Whichever group is right makes no difference to the day-to-day duty of Christians. Their common aim is to extend the rule of Christ in the world. Christ taught his followers to pray to God. "Thy kingdom come. Thy will be done, on earth as it is done in heaven." That is the supreme aim: God ruling on earth as in heaven.

It makes the heart ache with longing to think of what Christ could do in this world if men and women would submit to his rule. He would pull down the barriers of class, color, and race. The differences of political theories and religious creeds would be reconciled in his mind—which is all truth. He would stop the insane drift to war, and make the human race the family of his Father in heaven. Racial equality, economic justice, political freedom, and world peace are all involved in the family ideal.

The evil and selfishness in men hinder him. He is impeded, also, by a lack of boldness in his Church. It is the bias of Church leaders in all lands to lean towards the policy of the leaders of their State, and Church divisions prevent the Church speaking Christ's word to the world above the level of the quarrelling nations.

Christ is the real though unrecognized world authority. He said himself, "All authority has been given to me in heaven and in earth." (Matt. 28:18.) If men and women would recognize that authority, if they would commit their lives to him, if they would allow him to deal with their radical selfishness and unite under his direction, the fulfillment of the prayer would come and God's will be done on earth as it is done in heaven.

EPILOGUE

100

So What?

WE BEGAN BY SAYING THAT NO ONE WAS EVER ARGUED INTO RE-
ligion, and we end by repeating it. The gain of talking things
out is that it clears the runway of obstacles which need not be
there, but it is up to the man himself to start the engine of his
plane and take off.

What are you going to do about it? There are still the three
possibilities we mentioned. You can deny all deep meaning to
life and insist that we are only clever animals, that when we
die we shall go into the earth and rot. Or you can say, "I don't
know, and I don't think anybody else does. I'm going to live
in that uncertainty." Or you can answer the call of Christ who
says, "Follow Me"—start up the engine of the plane, and take
off on a great adventure.

Picture Christ standing before you for a moment. Without
the slightest disrespect to the other great religious leaders of the
world, he is a person apart. See him entering life in the stable
at Bethlehem, growing up in a poor home in Nazareth, bending
over the bench till he was thirty, moving out into the wider life
of his people, and teaching, healing, helping all who come to
him, until they drag him to death as a man not fit to live. He
dies praying for his murderers' pardon.

Think of his influence on the world. Recognize that most
things of worth in our life stem from him, and ask yourself
whether he is not the brightest light we have in this gray world.

Is it stupid or wise (in the position in which we find ourselves) to follow the best that we know? It is Christ or the dark.

Take off. Give God a chance. Begin to pray. Talk it over with a friend who is a convinced Christian, and to whom it would be easy to open your mind. There is almost certainly a friendly parson in the neighborhood with whom you could discuss your difficulties unhurriedly and "man-to-man." You can't really do this on your own. You need the Church. And the best time is *now*.

A good flight to you—and happy landing!